WHAT LEADERS ARE SAYING ABOUT
THE BRAVE:

A friend told me, "The easiest way to share the good news is to tell YOUR story!" Everyone has a story, and what makes it so powerful is that it's YOUR own personal experience that no one could really devalue. Others benefit from hearing the message of truth known in YOUR heart and mind. Michaels' story, along with a taste of encouragement of many slices from the fruit of the Spirit of God, fills our hearts with such value now and forever!

Lee Rouson
Principal Executor, Move Your Chains, Consulting Team
Two Time Super Bowl Champion, New York Football Giants
Flanders, New Jersey

The Brave is the real deal: transparent and heart-searching, just like the author himself. For those who want an authentic picture of redemption in action, this book is for you. But be ready for a staggering journey into God's transformative grace, and the inescapable challenge to experience it for yourself.

Mark Nigro
Executive Pastor of Cornerstone Church and Christian Entrepreneur
Howell, New Jersey

In a word, honesty. Michael's story is intended to inspire other men to be honest and live lives identified in Christ. His experiences will build your courage, shape your perspective, and strengthen your sense of purpose as you discover your identity in Christ. It's a straightforward, no fluff, thought-provoking book that's applicable to every man's life.

Dustin Whitson
Senior Pastor of Calvary Chapel Conference Center
Washington, Utah

Authentic! I've known Michael for many years and have been blessed to see much of his journey firsthand. Many men will be blessed and challenged by the truths in these pages. It is clear that the grace of God has transformed not just Michael but his whole family—and I pray God will transform many more through the vulnerability and authenticity of this book.

Mike McCarrick
Senior Pastor of Cornerstone Church
Howell, New Jersey

What a perfect name for this book—*The Brave*! It's Real, Raw, and Honest. Michael's story reveals not only his brokenness, but ours as well, and God's redemptive plan to use our pain for His purpose. My wife and I have been blessed to walk with the Bowens through the journey of his amazing transformation. In this book, you will find real power, encouragement, and direction for a life of clear purpose and freedom.

Dr. Ron Eccles
Founder of ROAR and author of *Unstoppable Christian* and *Going Vertical Coaching*
Bradenton, Florida

This book is an absolute must-read! In a society where the truth of our real identity in Christ is masked by a veneer of success, Michael shatters all pretenses by giving us a raw and honest front-row view of his journey from rock bottom to redemption. I know Michael personally. He doesn't just preach it. He's a true warrior whose life exemplifies his profession of faith. Buy ten copies, keep one, and pass along the rest! You'll be glad you did!

Samuel Park
Senior Pastor of Truth Church and Christian Entrepreneur
Centennial, Colorado

Michael's book, *The Brave*, is an incredible testimony of a man's dedication to lean into God and press forward. He is an awesome example of who you can become when you learn to hear God's voice and are obedient to follow Him. Michael is becoming a mighty man of God, an incredible husband, father, leader, and example for other men.

This book will be instrumental in moving men into a true and lasting relationship with God. *The Brave* is a very easy read with great tools included to move people to a new level of awareness of who they are in Christ.

Dave Dudley
Christian Business Owner
Rosemount, Minnesota

This book is a powerful story of the struggles and failures in a warrior's life, and how he was able to overcome. Michael is very humble and vulnerable as he shares his life's journey. This is an interactive study that challenges each reader to evaluate his life and be the man God designed him to be.

Debbie Lee
CEO of America's Mighty Warrior and Proud Mother of Navy SEAL Marc Lee KIA 8-2-06
Surprise, Arizona

God created men. God loves men. God uses men. In this power-packed book, Michael gives us a glimpse of the inward work God wants to do in every man. As he shares the backdrop of the grace of God in transforming his life, he invites you into the same experience of God's grace. God created you. God loves you. God will use you. Jump in to your new exciting life with both feet. In the Old Testament, Joshua made a choice. Make the same one. As for your house, choose to serve the Lord!

Ed Taylor
Pastor of Calvary Chapel Aurora
Aurora, Colorado
edtaylor.org

Jesus said that it is not the healthy who need a doctor, but the sick, and that He didn't come to call the righteous, but the sinner to repentance. Yet many Christian men still walk around wearing a mask and trying so hard to avoid revealing the broken places in their hearts because they're afraid of being rejected by God and other people. This book is about shedding the mask and allowing God to do what He came to do: restore the broken soul. Mike shows us by way of example. He bravely shares his journey of how shedding his own mask has led to healing and restoration, and he invites us to do the same by providing a very scriptural blueprint for us. This is a very well-written book that will inspire you to live more transparently before God and others.

Cody Whittaker
Missionary and Church Planter
Ibarra, Ecuador

The Brave

Becoming men of honor,
integrity, strength, and grace

MICHAEL BOWEN

ISBN:
Print 978-1-947505-36-0
Digital 978-1-947505-37-7

Cover design and interior formatting by Anne McLaughlin, Blue Lake Design
Photo of Michael on back cover by Ryanne Cooksey
Published by Baxter Press
Printed in the United States

I want to dedicate the book to my wife Sung,

a mighty woman of God,

our kids—Arthur, Bradley, Tehya, Caleb and Micalah,

and our grandkids—Benjamin, Jack and Adelaide.

Contents

Foreword

This book is about men, for men, by a man's man. Michael is one of the most honest, courageous men I've ever known. Walking with Jesus isn't just a concept to him. He's "all in" with God, his family, his church, his friends, and his business. But don't get me wrong: Michael isn't an over-the-top, wild-eyed radical. He's vulnerable without being weak, strong without being pushy, wise without being a know-it-all, and always on the journey, knowing God's not finished with him yet.

When Michael came to our church, I had the opportunity to observe his impact on other men. He's bold and creative, but he's the consummate team player. He didn't show up and say, "Step aside and watch me. I'll show you how to reach and disciple men." Instead, he looked for his place within what we were already doing, supporting our mission, advancing our purpose, and building on our vision. He got involved with the men at our church as a learner, a peer, and a friend. He expected these men to shape him every bit as much (or more) than he would shape them. I told a friend, "Michael is exactly the kind of guy every pastor is looking for!"

Since I've known him, I've been impressed with his open heart to learn and grow. The stories, biblical principles, and applications you'll find in this book were forged in the fire of Michael's personal experience. There's no fluff here. He's brutally honest about his sins, his hurts and disappointments, and his failures, but there's no self-pity and no blaming others. In each of these stories, he shares how God met him and used those difficult moments to teach him the most important lessons of his life.

Some leaders and authors describe their success in ways that may be amazing, but they don't connect with real people with real problems and real dreams. Michael doesn't put himself on a pedestal . . . he's one of us. As I read the manuscript of *The Brave*, I felt like I was listening to a gifted player-coach, someone who is still in the game and is devoted to help men take steps forward. Other experts may say, "Follow my system," but Michael is saying, "Follow my example."

A man's reputation is supremely valuable . . . and it's usually an accurate reflection of his true character. The men in our church love and respect Michael. In fact, they have nothing but praise for his impact in their lives. They observed him up close in our men's ministry. They rubbed shoulders with him in meetings and in informal gatherings. As the pastor of a large church, I don't get close enough to very many people for them to become sandpaper to me, rubbing off the rough spots and smoothing out the sharp edges, but Michael has been sandpaper in the lives of many men in our church, and now in his home in Colorado. To a man, they've told me in one way or another, "He's the real deal!" I'm not sure there's anything better that can be said about a Christian man, husband, father, and friend.

No matter where you are in your spiritual journey, this book is for you. If you're just checking out faith in Christ and don't want to hang around inauthentic people, you'll love this book. God may use it to open your heart to a real faith in Him. If you're a believer but you feel sidetracked by broken dreams, failures, or boredom, God may use Michael's stories to inspire you to dream again . . . and dream big. And if you're full-on and full-out for Jesus, you'll find a running partner in Michael—and I hope you can keep up!

I believe God has something for you in the pages of Michael's book. As you begin reading, ask God to make himself real to you . . . maybe more real than you've ever imagined before. That's my prayer for you.

Rob Ketterling
Lead Pastor of River Valley Church, Minneapolis, Minnesota

CHAPTER 1

The Unlikely

Fight the good fight of the faith. Take hold of the eternal
life to which you were called and about which you made
the good confession in the presence of many witnesses.

–1 Timothy 6:12

> Alleged impossibilities are opportunities for our capabilities
> to be stretched.
>
> –Chuck Swindoll

When I was a freshman in high school, the walls of my life were
crumbling around me. My parents divorced, and it wasn't a
friendly end to their marriage. My father had been a Force
RECON Marine, conducting amphibious reconnaissance in
Vietnam to determine the best ground for upcoming assaults.
He loved the *Godfather* movies, and he looked amazingly like the
Don himself, Vito Corleone. In fact, I was born about the time
the first movie was released in 1972, and I'm named after the godfather's son, Michael, and Michael's son, Anthony. I guess you
could say that my dad was "really into the movie." Like the godfather, my dad had a rough background, so he always dressed in
the finest clothes to look the part of the man everyone respected
. . . and feared.

My dad was a violent man. He was verbally cruel and physically harsh. When I was a little boy and got out of line, he beat me. Very soon, it only took "that look" to put me back in my place. If I didn't react quickly, I knew what was coming. Just before my parents split up, my older sister and my dad got into an argument one morning. When my mother tried to defend my sister, Dad started poking her in the face. She had just had surgery on her broken nose, so it really hurt her. My sister jumped on his back to try to get him to stop, but he turned his wrath on her and beat her badly. I grabbed my two little brothers, who were four and six, and took them into the backyard. I was the protector, a role that would surface again and again in my life. My sister went to school and told her teacher what had happened, and a few hours later, the police came, handcuffed my dad, and took him to jail. I knew this wouldn't end well. He wasn't the humble, sorrowful, repenting type. My parents had split up several times before, and each time he cut off all financial support to punish her for not being cooperative enough. We barely scraped by each time, and this promised to be another lean time in our house. This time, though, he didn't come back. It was the last straw in their very tense, violent, and loveless marriage.

Before the arrest and the final breakup, my mother had been very withdrawn to protect herself, and the divorce only caused her to go further into her shell. She reverted back to old coping mechanisms to numb the pain, and consequently, she had very little emotional support to offer her four children. Like countless other wives and mothers in similar difficult situations, she tried her best.

THE ASSESSMENT

Like many kids who come from similar family backgrounds, I went into full-fledged rebellion—doing everything a responsible, loving parent wouldn't want a teenaged son to do. I spent most of my time with older boys who were at least two grades ahead of me in school. They were my role models and my surrogate parents. I didn't have any form of faith that could be an anchor for me. I had been told we were Methodists, but that label meant nothing to me. My father had a Jewish heritage, with some Catholicism stirred into the pot. I was really confused about God and life. I thought that if I didn't eat meat on Friday and I went to church on Sunday, I could do anything I wanted the rest of the week. My Jewish and Catholic influences gave me rules, but I didn't even follow them. My Methodist teachings assured me of God's forgiveness, but I had never experienced it.

I was cutting school quite a bit, and when I went to class, I seldom had completed the assignments. All of this is the background for what happened in my ninth grade math class. For most of the kids in the classroom, I'm sure it was just another normal day, but I was worried about what was going to happen to Mom and us kids since Dad cut us off from any funds. My mother had already started seeing someone else, but I didn't know if he would treat her or the four of us any better than Dad did. As you might imagine, I hated authority figures because I felt betrayed by them. In class that day, I was sitting about three rows back, consumed by my anxious thoughts, when my teacher told everyone, "Turn in your algebra homework."

I had been so preoccupied with all the drama in our family that I hadn't even glanced at the assignment. I only went to school to hang out around my friends. I needed them . . . I didn't need algebra. The other kids turned in their papers, but I just sat there. My teacher scanned the room and then said, "Mr. Bowen, come up to my desk." When I got there, he growled, "Where is your assignment?"

I shrugged, "I didn't do it."

He narrowed his eyes and told me, "This is a repetitive thing with you. You've missed a lot of assignments this year." He paused for a second and then gave his final assessment of me: "Mr. Bowen, you'll never amount to anything!" He let that sink in, and then he said with a look of disgust, "If I had to vote right now, you'd be 'the least likely to succeed.'"

"Mr. Bowen, you'll never amount to anything!"

Of course, everyone in the room heard this exchange. I'm not sure how he expected me to respond, but I started laughing and walked back to my desk. I wanted the rest of the kids to believe that the teacher's condemnation didn't bother me one bit, but it did . . . it rocked my world. Actually, this was a carbon copy of the way I'd responded to the chaos and blame in our family—I tried to act like it didn't bother me and laugh it off, but each event was another knife wound in my soul.

TWO LESSONS

Over the years of reflecting on how my family experiences shaped me, I remembered a time when I was six years old on a visit to my grandmother in Deal, New Jersey. My uncle, my father's half-brother, spent a lot of time with me that summer. We went to the beach, went fishing, and had more than our share of ice cream. One day when I was hanging out with him, we went with six or seven other guys to paint the house of the mother of one of his friends. My uncle was eighteen years old, and someone had brought a keg of beer for the day. As they climbed ladders and painted siding and railing, I was the designated "beer gopher." Every time I filled up a plastic cup for one of them, I took a sip or two.

In the early afternoon, my uncle was on a ladder, and he asked me to bring him a gallon bucket of paint. I went up a few steps, lost my balance and fell back to the ground—the paint spilled all over me. My uncle scampered down the ladder, wiped paint out of my eyes, and stared at me. He asked, "Michael, are you drunk?"

The other boys heard him, and they were quite amused. "Your nephew is lit!" "That little guy tried to keep up with us. That's so cool." "Little Michael is wasted!"

My uncle found a hose and sprayed the paint off me. (I'm glad it was latex.) He took my clothes inside to wash them out in a sink. A few minutes later, he came out and told the others, "That's it for today, guys." They cleaned their brushes and put away the paint, and they left. My uncle put my wet clothes in the car. With me in my underwear, he went through the drive-thru at McDonalds and got me something to eat. Then he drove around long enough for the alcohol to wear off before taking me back to my grandmother's house. Finally, my clothes dried and I put them on. Before we got out of the car, he told me, "Don't say a word about all this, or your dad will kill me!" We walked in and told them about painting the house . . . with not a word about the keg, the spilled paint, or sobering me up.

I certainly couldn't articulate it, but I internalized a lesson that day: No matter what has happened, I can clean up my outside, lie, and act like everything is just fine . . . and get away with it.

Two years later, our family was living in southwest Philadelphia near the airport, and I had a good friend, Tommy, a rough Italian kid. We were in the second grade. Every day, Tommy and I walked almost a mile on the sidewalk next to a busy highway, Chester Pike, to Sharon Hill Elementary School. One morning, when we were about halfway to school, we decided to wait until his mom left the house for work. Our brilliant plan was to go back to the house to do whatever adults did when there were no kids around. Tommy's father had an elaborate bar downstairs with all kinds of liquor. We had failed to realize, however, that though his mother wasn't home, lots of Italian mothers and grandmothers lived nearby, and they kept a sharp eye out for anything unusual—like two eight-year-old boys playing hooky.

We were in the basement mixing whatever looked interesting to us, and no matter how bad it tasted, we drank it. We thought we were hot stuff! About an hour later, we heard footsteps. One of the ladies in the neighborhood had called Tommy's mom at the bank where she worked. Needless to say, she wasn't too happy when she got to the house. She escorted us to school and ushered us into the principal's office. I remember his name was Mr. Schumacher. (Isn't it funny what sticks in your mind from memorable childhood moments?) When Tommy's mother told him what we'd done, he pulled a big paddle out of his desk and laid into us. It was bad, but it wasn't a death blow. That came a few hours later when my dad got home.

It may have been the embarrassment he felt that his son had skipped school, and worse, got caught, but the beating from him was the worst I'd ever endured. It seemed it would never end. When it was finally over, I ran to my room. I couldn't stop crying, and I was shaking uncontrollably. My mother walked in with a half an anti-anxiety pill and told me to take it. In a few minutes, I felt numb and went to sleep. I learned another lesson that day: If I take a pill, my physical and emotional pain will go away, and I'll feel better. (That certainly wasn't a positive, constructive message during my emotional growth cycle!)

A NEW HEADING

By the time I was sixteen, the trauma of the divorce had taken its toll. We were living in Wilmington, Delaware, and I had dropped out of high school, but before long, my mom decided to leave with my two little brothers to live near Denver with her sister. With her settlement, mom bought her "divorce car," a two-seater Mazda RX-7. She had four children, which tells you a lot about her frame of mind at the time. She asked me to drive her car to Colorado by myself because she and my brothers were going to fly. I put a few clothes in a duffle bag, loaded up my cassette tapes, and hit the road. I'd spent most of my childhood with older kids, so I'd always found a way to figure things out. Mom gave me $200 for gas and food. Since I wasn't eighteen, I couldn't rent hotel rooms, so I went to cheap hotels, handed the attendant $50, and asked if I could have a room off the books for the night. It worked every time.

When I got to Colorado, Aunt Wendy took me aside and said, "Michael, your mom is trying to start over, to make something of her life. I think you might want to start over, too." That's exactly what it felt like: a new start. I was away from my dad, away from my old friends, and away from all the crazy stuff we'd been doing. I was ready to walk a different path. When I looked in the mirror, I knew I needed to start by getting in better shape. I stopped smoking and started running. I soon realized I wasn't going anywhere without a high school diploma, so I began studying for my GED. Only a few months later, I sat for my GED at Arapahoe Community College, and I passed. Things were looking up.

My dad wasn't happy that Mom had moved to Colorado with my two brothers and me. He accused her of kidnapping and filed a lawsuit. Before long, he won his suit, and we had to move back to live near him—which shook all of us to our core. In Colorado, we had found safety and hope for the future with my aunt, and now we had to be near the source of so much chaos, drama, and pain. Our time in the refuge was over. I drove Mom's car back to Delaware where she rented a two-bedroom apartment.

By this time, I was seventeen. I didn't want to be a burden to my mother, so I moved into the studio apartment of a friend named Joe and got a job at a high-end restaurant in downtown Wilmington. My new start soon began running off the rails, and the drinking and drugging returned.

One morning I woke up and thought, *If I keep up this lifestyle, I won't make it to twenty-one.* I walked into a military recruiting office wearing pink shorts, flip flops, and a tank top, and I sported long surfer hair. I looked like Jeff Spicoli in *Fast Times at Ridgemont High*! The building housed the recruiting offices of the

Marines, Air Force, and Navy. As soon as the Marine looked at me, he started laughing. He asked, "So, you're thinking of being a Marine?" What a jerk. I sure wasn't going to talk to that guy. The Air Force recruiter told me they weren't accepting anyone with only a GED, so that was out. The lady in the Navy office told me the Navy had relaxed their requirements because the first Gulf War showed them their need for more recruits. She was so kind, wise, and knowledgeable. She said, "Listen, I'm not going to ask you if you've done drugs. If you have, I suggest you wait thirty days to come back for your physical and the military battery tests." That was really good advice.

I stopped drinking and using, got a haircut, put on some regular clothes, and showed up a month later at the recruiting office. I took the battery of tests, passed, had a physical, passed the drug test, and joined the Navy. My main motivation was to prove all the people who doubted me wrong, especially my math teacher.

My life immediately changed from no structure to all structure, and I loved it. A lot of the guys complained about the rigors of boot camp, but to me, it was easy compared to what I'd experienced in my family. And the benefits were fantastic: I had three good meals a day, clothes that fit, and my laundry was done for me. Before I joined, I had been working two jobs to help provide for my mom, my sister, and my brothers. While in high school, I worked at a gas station from 11 p.m. until 7 a.m., and then I went to school. I had another job after school until I went to the station. On the days I didn't work, I tried to catch up on my sleep. Compared to that, boot camp was a breeze.

Immediately after boot camp, my first assignment was as a recruiter assistant, and ironically, I was placed in my hometown and was able to visit the same high school where I'd dropped out. By this time, I was eighteen, wearing dress blues, walking down the halls, and talking to kids about joining the Navy. When people recognized me, I got some funny stares and plenty of questions. I sure couldn't answer very many of them . . . what did I know about serving in the Navy? Not much. I only knew that it was right where I wanted to be.

When I joined the Navy, I took a battery of tests to identify my aptitude for various roles, and I scored very well, which allowed me to have my pick at a multitude of available jobs. It's surprising that I did so well because I was a high school dropout who couldn't have cared less about my education. The Navy detailer (the equivalent of an HR director) asked me to pick a job I qualified for, and one of them was being a firefighter. That sounded perfect to me.

I was assigned to a welding and firefighting school at the Naval Shipyard near Broad Street in Philadelphia. I graduated in the top three of my class, which afforded me the opportunity to pick my next duty station. At this point I knew one thing for sure: I wanted to get as far from home as possible. The options for my assignment were Navy bases in Japan, Guam, and Hawaii. I couldn't speak Japanese, and I heard there are a lot of snakes in Guam, so I chose Hawaii. My mom loved to watch Tom Selleck in *Magnum P.I.*, so I had a pretty good idea what the islands looked like. I was stationed at Submarine Base Pearl Harbor. We trained hard, and I was assigned to work on nuclear-powered submarines. After I was in Hawaii for eighteen months, SEAL recruiters visited our command and asked me to consider entering their training program. I'll save that story for later in the book, but it's another important chapter in my life history.

TURNING POINT

By September 11, 2001, I had been out of the Navy for three years and was living in Freehold, New Jersey, working for my dad. Yes, that's right—working for my dad. I'd become friends with a guy named Tim. He was a tough guy, a Golden Gloves boxer. Every week, he knocked on the door of my apartment and asked me two questions . . . the same two questions every time: "Hey Michael, do you want to play on our hockey team?" I told him, "No, I don't play hockey." And "Do you want to go to church with me this Sunday?" I told him, "No, thanks."

One day Tim showed up with a big slash in his forehead. I asked, "What happened to you?"

He laughed and told me, "Somebody got me with a high stick." Without missing a beat, he asked, "Do you want to play hockey on our team?"

"Tim, in my job, I give presentations. I can't show up with a gash in my face! No, I'm not going to play hockey with you."

"Okay," he smiled. "Well, do you want to go to church with me this Sunday?"

For some reason, I said, "Yes, I want to. I *need* to." I don't know who was more surprised, Tim or me.

He picked me up on Sunday morning, and we went to a church called Calvary Chapel Old Bridge. At the end of the service, the pastor gave an invitation for people to come forward to receive Christ as their Savior and Lord. Up to that point, I knew nothing about the cross of Jesus, but that morning, it made sense. Jesus died in my place. He took the penalty for my sins. Because of His sacrifice, I could be forgiven and become a child of God. When I got to the altar, I was weeping. I experienced the love of God in a way that I'd never dreamed possible.

I've never looked back, but being born again doesn't instantly erase years of emotional wounds and twisted thinking. The process of following Jesus inevitably includes magnificent ups and soul-crushing downs . . . and God teaches important lessons in every moment and every circumstance. As we increasingly understand what it means to give up our selfishness and let the love of God empower and direct us, we're gradually (very gradually) transformed internally in our desires and affections and externally as we follow Jesus' example to lay down our lives for others. This book is about that process.

TWIN TRAITS

To describe what it means to be a Christian man in our culture, we need to look no further than the example of Jesus. As we read the Gospels, we see a man who was sure of His calling, decisive without oppressing those around Him, courageous in the face of fierce opposition, and exquisitely tender with people who were in need. The twin traits I see in Him are courage and humility—both, not one or the other. Jesus is, at the same time, the Lion of Judah and the Lamb of God. These are the same qualities we see in the stories of every person who has won the Bronze Star, the Silver Star, the Distinguished Service Cross, the Medal of Honor, and every other award for heroism. These soldiers, sailors, and airmen were willing to risk their lives—and often give their lives—for others. I admire these people for their courage propelled by humility.

Currently, the secular world is having a very difficult time understanding what it means to be a man. Traditional characteristics of men, like boldness and toughness, are being examined more closely, and the news is filled with stories of men using their power to oppress or abuse others. But that's only one picture (or actually, a misrepresentation) of what it means to be a man.

Jesus is, at the same time, the Lion of Judah and the Lamb of God.

Writers like Jim Collins have a much better concept of manhood. He describes "Level 5 Leaders" in his groundbreaking book, *Good to Great*. Collins and his research team analyzed the success or failure of companies across a wide variety of industries, and they found a handful— eleven to be exact—that were transformed from "good" to "great." He and his team made a surprising discovery: in each of these outstanding companies, the leaders were very different from all the others they studied. In an article in *Harvard Business Review*, Collins explains:

> Our discovery of Level 5 leadership is counterintuitive. Indeed, it is countercultural. People generally assume that transforming companies from good to great requires larger-than-life leaders—big personalities like Iacocca, Dunlap, Welch, and Gault, who make headlines and become celebrities. . . . Level 5 leaders are a study in duality: modest and willful, shy and fearless. To grasp this concept, consider Abraham Lincoln, who never let his ego get in the way of his ambition to create an enduring great nation. Author Henry Adams called him

"a quiet, peaceful, shy figure." But those who thought Lincoln's understated manner signaled weakness in the man found themselves terribly mistaken—to the scale of 250,000 Confederate and 360,000 Union lives, including Lincoln's own.

Collins was asked if the dual qualities of humility and courage can be learned or acquired. He answered:

> My preliminary hypothesis is that there are two categories of people: those who don't have the Level 5 seed within them and those who do. The first category consists of people who could never in a million years bring themselves to subjugate their own needs to the greater ambition of something larger and more lasting than themselves. . . . The second category consists of people who could evolve to Level 5; the capability resides within them, perhaps buried or ignored or simply nascent. Under the right circumstances—with self-reflection, a mentor, loving parents, a significant life experience, or other factors—the seed can begin to develop.[1]

This is a picture in the business world of what every Christian man is called to become in every aspect of life. As Collins mentions, perhaps it's buried or ignored or just beginning to appear, but the seed can be planted, watered, and nurtured so that it becomes strong and fruitful.

A number of factors in our culture are making men weak and feeble. To be honest, quite a few of them—the #MeToo movement, for instance—are necessary correctives for male malfeasance, but I believe many of us have abdicated our God-given role in our families, our churches, our companies, and our communities. Author, consultant, and pastor Joseph Mattera has identified "The Signs of an Emotionally Emasculated Man." These include:

- Abdicating leadership to wives and even children.
- Allowing choices to be dictated by fear, hurt, anger, or shame.
- Second-guessing decisions.
- Failing to be the spiritual leader in marriage and the family.
- Using anger to mask insecurities.
- Fleeing, fighting, or freezing to avoid dealing with conflict.[2]

A clear, biblical identity is the antidote to gender uncertainty and role reversals. More than ever, men need to be men . . . but we need to be more like Jesus, not Rambo! We're warriors, but we're protectors; strong and compassionate; tough and tender. Biblical manhood isn't weakness at all. It's a product of massive inner strength, which gives us the stability to take the risk to be completely honest about our sins and flaws. Only secure, forgiven people can get outside themselves to genuinely care for others. Insecure people are compelled to control others and hide from painful truths, and when their mask finally doesn't work any longer, they give up on making a difference.

All my life, I've wanted to be a warrior/protector. I joined the Navy, chose to be a firefighter, and entered SEAL training because those skills offered the opportunity to fulfill my dream.

My background certainly shaped my desires. I wasn't bullied at school, but I often got into fights because of the intense anger that came from being bullied at home. As I was growing up, my dad was the consummate tough guy, and during my important childhood years, he had no capacity to demonstrate love, kindness, patience, and affection. My heart to care for people is the unexpected consequence of not being cared for by the one whose love and protection I needed most.

Into that vacuum, Tim stepped in. A champion boxer, hockey player, and huge man, he showed up at my door week after week to invite me to join him on the ice and at church. I assumed Christian men wore ugly suits, couldn't lift fifty pounds, were perpetually sour, and talked about things nobody (especially me) cared about. Tim smashed that stereotype. The gash on his forehead didn't faze him one bit. He was secure enough to show up again, and finally, I responded to his invitation . . . and Christ's.

Right after I trusted in Jesus, Tim introduced me to some guys he had joined for a men's Bible study. They didn't know me, but they welcomed me. One of them said, "We meet every Thursday night at Mark Henry's house." But that wasn't all he said. "If you can go to a bar on Thursday night, you can come to our Bible Study. If you don't come on your own, we'll drop by your apartment and get you. No excuses."

He didn't even know me . . . but he knew me. I was a master at making up excuses to avoid things I didn't want to do, but if someone offered me a ticket to a ball game, I cleared my schedule so I could go. My go-to excuse was that I was "too busy," but that wasn't going to fly with these guys. They're real men who were (and still are) deeply committed to walk with Jesus all day every day.

Of course, I was very guarded during the first meeting or two, but my walls began to come down when Mark showed us a fifteen-minute video of Dick Hoyt, who had been a Lieutenant Colonel in the Air National Guard, and whose son Rick was confined to a wheelchair with cerebral palsy. Dick wasn't content to let his son waste away in a sterile room. He pushed Rick in over 1,100 races, including thirty-two Boston Marathons, an Ironman Triathlon, and a 3,735-mile trek across America over forty-five days. In the video, Dick's obvious love for his son, and Rick's grateful appreciation for his father's tender care, moved all of us. We cried like little kids . . . even me. I thought, *Wait a minute! We're men. We're not supposed to cry!* But it was the only appropriate response to this beautiful story of redemption, compassion, and affection. The video obviously meant a lot to the other guys, but it was especially meaningful to me. Dick was giving his son something I hadn't gotten from my dad. And of course, we talked about the connection to the gospel—that the Father loves us, who are so disfigured and crippled by sin—with boundless, exuberant, joyful affection.

I met these men years ago, but today, all of them are making a difference in the lives of others. One of them is an author and filmmaker, and Mark is a boxing coach, mentor, and unofficial chaplain for UFC fighters—he's seeing some of the toughest guys in the sport come to Christ. Lonnie is a soft-spoken journalist, athlete, and business owner. As I spent time around them, I realized they were as diverse as the twelve men who were Jesus' disciples—from very different backgrounds and with very different personalities, but with a similar heart for God. Like Tim, they all shattered my stereotype of Christian men. They weren't weak, and they weren't feeble. They're funny and compassionate, secure and kind, tenacious and great listeners—and above all, they're ruthlessly honest about their struggles to be true to their commitment to Jesus.

MY HOPE FOR YOU

In countless conversations with men over the past couple of decades since I became a Christian, I've had the privilege to know some people who are committed to become more like Jesus—as fierce as a lion but as humble as a lamb. But I've also noticed two patterns that aren't taking men where they really want to go. Some men have avoided relationships with other men who are strong enough to be honest. Many of them avoid strong, honest men completely by staying away, but others get near without being open. You know what I mean. Without a bedrock security of knowing they're loved, forgiven, and accepted, they "put on a face" to present themselves as "put together." They don't want anyone to know about the doubts, questions, and desires they harbor . . . because they're afraid that if people knew, they'd run away, laugh, or mock them as hypocrites. But they *are* hypocrites because they're presenting themselves as something they aren't. They need to find a group, or at least one wise friend, who will be a mentor and help them unpack the pain of the past or tear down the walls that are preventing them from moving forward.

Another group of men have a different (but equally ineffective) solution to their hidden struggles. They may have tried to fool people before, but no longer. They've given up, bailed out, quit the game. They're deeply discouraged, and they see no hope for meaningful change.

I've found that God wants to use our deepest wounds and our biggest flaws to shape us into something that reflects His strength and love. Hey, if He can do it in my life, He can do it in anyone's. But I'm not unique . . . not by a long shot. The past doesn't have to be the rocks where our lives are shipwrecked. Our past can become a rock of renewal, forgiveness, and hope, but only if we find the courage to be honest about it. When we try to convince ourselves that past hurts haven't affected us or they didn't even happen, we're living a lie . . . and the lie becomes a fortress of shame that crushes our spirits, robs us of purpose, and steals our joy.

If you'd taken a good look at me when I was a young man, you probably would have concluded that it was highly unlikely that I'd make it in life. As a matter of fact, I thought for sure I'd be dead before my 21st birthday. I was told I'd never amount to anything, and my parents didn't correct that negative perception by communicating any confidence in me. That was the toxic conclusion I lived with for a long time, and it has been my biggest battle both as a Christian and even as a success in business. I had to die to the lie.

I had to die to the lie.

In his second letter to the Christians in Corinth, Paul explained that the battle for our hearts is like siege warfare: "For though we walk in the flesh, we are not waging war according to the flesh. For the weapons of our warfare are not of the flesh but have divine power to destroy strongholds. We destroy arguments and every lofty opinion raised against the knowledge of God, and take every thought captive to obey Christ" (2 Corinthians 10:3-5).

Some of our group are fighting battles against alcoholism, drug addiction, gambling, or pornography; all of us are fighting lust for women (and maybe men), money, or prestige; and some are fighting the hardest battle, the one against self-righteousness, thinking we don't have big problems like "those guys." My point is that all of us are in a battle. It may look different for each of us, but we're not empty-handed. We have the power of the truth in God's Word, the power of the Spirit who can work all things in us and for us, and the power of authentic friendships with men who challenge us and support us.

My hope is that you'll find these sources of power as you read this book.

At the end of each chapter, you'll find some questions to help you reflect on the principles in the chapter and stimulate discussion with some men you trust. This isn't a timed test, so don't hurry through the questions. Take your time and think about them prayerfully, honestly, and courageously. Trust God to do a great work in your heart. He really wants to.

THINK ABOUT IT:

1. How can men tell if they're haunted by past wounds and sins?

2. What's the process to transform those negative experiences into something positive, redemptive, and wonderful?

3. Some people say that the hurts we suffer in the first half of our lives become our platform for effective influence for the rest

of our lives. Do you agree or disagree with this statement? Explain your answer.

4. How would you define or describe "biblical manhood"?

5. Who do you know who models a life of courage and humility? What is the impact of that person on you and others?

6. Look at 2 Corinthians 10:3-5 again. How is our battle like siege warfare?

7. What do you hope to get out of this book?

CHAPTER 2

The Uncommon

Then Jesus told his disciples, "If anyone would come after me, let him deny himself and take up his cross and follow me. For whoever would save his life will lose it, but whoever loses his life for my sake will find it. For what will it profit a man if he gains the whole world and forfeits his soul? Or what shall a man give in return for his soul?"

—Matthew 16:24-26

> Above all, don't lie to yourself. The man who lies to himself and listens to his own lie comes to a point that he cannot distinguish the truth within him, or around him, and so loses all respect for himself and for others. And having no respect he ceases to love.
>
> —Novelist Fyodor Dostoevsky

Over the course of my life, I've worn several masks to hide the truth from people.

THE MASK I WORE IN THE NAVY

When I was a boy growing up in our home, I tried to project confidence on the outside while I was inwardly terrified and insecure. When I joined the Navy, I realized no one knew about my past. I had a clean slate, and I could tell any story that made me look good. The problem, of course, was that the gaping wound in my heart was still a reality. I tried to numb the pain with alcohol and drugs, and I tried to mask it by coming across as strong and desirable in my relationships with women. My only guardrail to keep me from going too far out of bounds was that I wanted to protect my career. At every evaluation, I received commendations. Each time, I felt good, I felt satisfied, I felt known and appreciated. I was rapidly advancing, and by the time I was twenty, I'd already been promoted to E-5, Petty Officer 2nd Class. Sailors who had been in the service for fifteen years reported to me, a kid who had been a high school dropout only a short time before. I was moving up, and I wasn't going to do anything that would jeopardize that!

In 1997, I was stationed in the Persian Gulf boarding and inspecting vessels to look for weapons of mass destruction. I had gotten married a few years before, but the relationship was rocky from the beginning. While on deployment, our command received a call from our homeport where my wife lived with our one-year-old, Bradley, and our nine-year-old, Arthur, whom my wife had from a previous marriage. There had been some violence reported, and our command ordered me back stateside to try to sort it all out . . . or they were going to take our kids into protective custody. A day later, I was on a plane from Kuwait back to Seattle. Thankfully, we arrived at a solution so the boys weren't taken, but I discovered some other problems that years later led to a separation and divorce. When all that was settled, I flew back to the Gulf, but I decided it was time to leave my military career to care for our boys.

THE MASK OF THE SMART STUDENT
AND TALENTED BUSINESSMAN

I left the Navy and entered college. I was working at the same time, wearing sharp suits and looking like the picture of a successful young man. Actually, I was a sales rep for my father's company in New Jersey and going to school at night. The decision to work for him was the product of a choice I'd made long before. Early in my naval career, I made a decision that I wasn't going to take sides between my mom and my dad. They both had plenty of faults, and I didn't want to get in the middle of their fight. I wasn't a boy any longer, and I wasn't dependent on them. I was a sailor in the U.S. Navy, and proud of it. I called my dad from a pay phone at my first assignment at Submarine Base Pearl Harbor. A year before, I had to ask him for permission to enlist because I wasn't yet eighteen, but I hadn't talked to him since then. When he answered, I said, "Dad, I'm stationed in Hawaii, and I want you to know that I've come to some decisions. I'm not going to get involved in the disputes between you and Mom. I didn't like you when I was growing up, but I want to look past all that and start over with you. If you want to get together and build a better relationship, I'm in." I traveled back to New Jersey a few times to meet with him, and he was occasionally in Hawaii when he had meetings with clients in the airline industry. I no longer needed him, and I was no longer afraid of him, so he couldn't control me with his anger. Amazingly, the change was good for both of us, and he craved spending time with me. We treated each other like we were old friends.

After my divorce, I shared custody of Arthur and Bradley, so when people looked at me, I made sure they saw a loving single dad who was outstanding in business and excelling in college. My neighbors, clients, and classmates saw a confident, sharply dressed, affectionate dad—they didn't see all the emotional turmoil just under the surface. I was a classic overachiever. I had to make the highest grade in my classes, win the biggest account for the company, and show up at all of my sons' events—and look great doing it all.

THE MASK I WORE AS A CHRISTIAN

When I became a Christian, I loved being with Tim and the other men in the Bible study, but my mask was still stuck on tight. I'd lived my entire life projecting an image, and change didn't come easily or quickly. Like everything else I've ever done, I was radically committed to Christ and the church. Before long, my pastor asked me to lead the youth ministry with his son Mike, and soon after that, I was invited to join the board of a church. I was driven, moving up, and overachieving in a new area of my life.

I needed help . . . and I wanted
help, but I didn't think I could tell
anyone what was going on.
It would blow my reputation
sky high!

The pressure was enormous, and I tried to cope in the same way I'd coped before, but instead of drinking, drugs, and sex, I was consumed with work while ignoring my family. I was living a lie. Yes, you remember correctly that I had been in a group that was ruthlessly honest, but I'd moved on, and I failed to internalize the lessons I'd learned with them. I wondered how I could give my life to Christ but still struggle with all these sins. I needed help . . . and I wanted help, but I didn't think I could tell anyone what was going on. It would blow my reputation sky high!

Sung and I had gotten married a few years earlier. She was a former Marine—very kind, but tough as nails. Like all married couples, we sometimes fought, but each of us brought a wealth of combat training to every disagreement. It rarely got nasty, but each time we argued, we fell back into old patterns of coping: I would avoid and she would shut down emotionally. Often, as we were navigating the early marriage blues, I went to church to lead the youth group. People asked, "Hey, Michael, how're you doing?" I invariably responded, "Terrific! Living the dream!" More lies.

God gave me some wake-up calls, but I hit the snooze button. Sung and I had trouble getting pregnant, and when she finally conceived, we found out she was carrying twins. We were so excited . . . until one of them died in utero. After she gave birth, she suffered from postpartum depression combined with the grief of losing a child. I was still leading, still preaching, still trying to look like nothing ever bothered me, and often neglecting to love and support my wife through her grief.

When kids are brought up in dysfunctional homes, their ability to trust gets messed up. Some try to cope by trusting even untrustworthy people, hoping that trusting them will earn enough points to win their love. Others don't trust anyone, and in trying to be invisible, become passive, indecisive, and meek.

They hope their withdrawal will signal that they're not a threat, and therefore, not a target of anyone's wrath. But some have the opposite reaction to their lack of trust; instead of withdrawing, they have to dominate, intimidate, and control every person and every situation. Is one response better than the others? No, none of these three types of mistrust leads to honesty, inner strength, and security. My lack of trust in people (and God) was a reflection of my relationship with my father. I couldn't depend on him to be both strong and kind, so I didn't believe God or anyone else would really be strong and kind to me. My mistrust created a type of prison, and I had thrown away the key. When I sensed the Holy Spirit prompting me to find someone to confide in, my response was an immediate, "No way! What will they think?"

There was rarely an event at the church that I wasn't right in the middle of. When the 7.0 earthquake devastated Haiti in 2010, we were living in Castle Rock, Colorado. The day after the disaster, my good friend Lonnie asked me to join him and his team to assist in the relief efforts. We flew with a group of men into the Dominican Republic with backpacks and tents, and we drove across the border into Haiti. We tried to help at an orphanage, but instead, we were sent to the home of a missionary couple, Cody and Maria Whittaker, who lived outside the city. We set up our tents and pitched in to do our part to rebuild buildings and lives. Before long, I made another trip down there with the team, and we became close to Cody and Maria. The next year, I had a business trip to Miami. I called Cody and asked if I could stay with them for a week to see what God was doing there through their gospel outreach and community involvement. He was glad to have me, but before he hung up, he said, "Michael, you need to know that there have been some home invasions around here in the past few weeks. Last week, a missionary was shot. It's not really safe."

My pride rose up, and I told him, "Come on, man! I'm ex-military. I'm not afraid of that stuff." I packed for both destinations, and after my meetings in Miami, I flew into Port-au-Prince.

From the moment Cody parked the car at his compound and we got out, I could tell Maria was on edge. She thought she saw a shadow moving or she heard strange noises. Fear does that to people. Maria was on high alert all week. Still, I thoroughly enjoyed those days with Cody. I wanted to make the last day count because I had to get up at 5:00 the next morning for the two-hour drive to the airport.

At about 2:00 in the morning, Cody came into my room and whispered, "Michael, get up."

I jumped wide awake, "Oh man, did I sleep through my alarm? I'm so sorry."

But Cody said, "No. Maria heard something."

I wanted to say, "Are you kidding me? How many times have we heard this all week?" But I didn't say it . . . because it was obvious Cody believed this time was different.

He whispered, "I heard it, too."

I reached over and opened a window. The house was surrounded by twelve-foot walls with barbed wire and broken glass embedded at the top. The compound had a heavy metal gate that seemed very secure. As I looked, I saw some shadows moving inside the walls. I hoped it was nothing, so I asked, "Do you have any animals out there?"

Cody shook his head. "No, our dog's in the house."

Then, I saw a distinct outline of a person. I'd like to say that I responded by dropping on my knees and asking for God's protection, but instead, I responded like the old sailor I'd been. I screamed threats and obscenities, trying scare off the intruders! By this time, Maria and the children were in the master bedroom. I told Cody, "They know we know they're out there, so their cover is blown. They'll leave."

Cody and I moved quietly into the living room toward the front door. He picked up a chair, and I grabbed one of the kid's scooters. Those were our weapons of choice. Suddenly, a window was smashed and gunshots rang out in the living room. I motioned to Cody to get on the floor and crawl back into the bedroom. Maria was freaking out. I told Cody and Maria to take the kids into a bathroom where there were no windows. She frantically tried to call the police station on her cell phone. I pushed the dresser against the door, put my back against it, and pressed my feet on a cinder block wall about three feet away.

We heard more glass break and more gunshots. Then an alarm went off. Cody opened the bathroom door and told me, "They're in the main courtyard. They're close!"

Maria was still trying to reach the police. The thieves had guns; I had a scooter behind a dresser. I heard the front door crash open and footsteps in the hall. They were only a few feet away now. I heard the doorknob turn, so I pressed my back against the dresser even harder. They pushed several times, but I held them off. I heard them speaking Creole, a language I'd never mastered. Then, gunshots came through the door. A lamp on the dresser shattered, and glass fell all over me. I felt an impact between my feet, but there was no pain.

Cody peaked out from the door and whispered, "We have to let them in. They'll kill us!"

I couldn't stand the thought of letting those thugs into the bedroom and watching them rape Cody's wife and little girl. I told him, "I'm not letting them in. No way!"

He nodded and then spoke loud enough for them to hear, "I'll give you anything you want, but you can't come into the bedroom."

They must have said "Okay" in Creole because Cody motioned for me to move the dresser. I told him, "After you go out there, I'm putting the dresser back against the door, and I'm not letting anyone in. Even if they kill you, I'm still not letting them in."

I moved the dresser out just a few inches, and Cody, who is really thin, squeezed through. He opened his safe and gave them the small amount of cash he had stashed in there. I heard Cody and the men yell at each other, and then I heard machine gun fire. I thought they'd killed him, but it was the police. They were firing warning shots as they drove toward the house.

Cody knocked on the bedroom door and yelled, "Let me back in!" The thieves ran as the police came into the house. We turned the lights on and saw the bullet holes in the dresser, the bed, and the walls. As I surveyed the scene, I realized one of the bullets had come through the dresser, passed four inches from my head, and struck the wall between my feet. It was a very close call.

Some other missionaries showed up with shotguns, a sign of support the police didn't appreciate. All of them got into an argument that I understood only because I'd seen those looks on people's faces before.

The assailants had gotten away with only $250 in cash, but they also took my iPad and my cell phone. Cody, Maria, and the children went to stay with some other missionaries while the police took a quick look at the damage. By this time, I needed to leave for the airport to catch my flight, but it was really hard to switch gears from a street fighter to casual missionary.

After the long ride, friends dropped me off at the airport at about 6:00 a.m. I borrowed a lady's phone to call Sung to tell her what had happened. Like me, she was both horrified and relieved. Then, I went to the makeshift Haitian airport bar and downed two rum and Cokes to calm my nerves. There has probably never been anyone so happy to get on a plane as I was that morning.

As soon as I landed, I was immersed back in business as usual. I tried to forget what happened in Haiti, but two weeks later, I was out for a run, and I felt like I was having a heart attack. When I got home and told Sung, she said, "You've lost all the color in your face. I'm taking you to the hospital."

I tried to tell her that I wasn't going to the hospital, but her insistence won the day. I had a battery of tests to determine what was wrong—heart, lungs, blood, the whole works. When the doctor finally walked in, he said, "Mr. Bowen, you had a panic attack." He prescribed an anti-anxiety medication, and it helped a lot. Over the next few months, I continued to experience panic attacks, so I kept taking the pills.

A few weeks later, I got a call that my dad's cancer had progressed, and he wasn't doing well at all. We immediately packed up our family and moved back to New Jersey to take care of dad and help with his business. I devoted myself to leading the company, and I put my service to God on hold. If anyone was interested, I told them I was a Christian, and I sometimes related the story about the attack in Haiti, but I was so busy that I didn't even go to church. I had never processed what happened that night with Cody and Maria, and my panic attacks were a symptom of posttraumatic stress disorder. I kept taking the pills to make it through each day.

My dad passed away, and now I shouldered the weight of his past business mistakes. To the casual observer, his company looked successful, but it was deep in debt. When I realized the severity of the financial problems, I became a workaholic determined to single-handedly save the day. At one point, I realized my life was out of control, largely because I was taking far, far too many anti-anxiety pills. I dumped them into the toilet. I was done with them. When I told Sung, she worried that I might have an adverse withdrawal effect because I quit too quickly, but I wasn't willing to take one more pill.

Sung looked at me and asked sadly, "How in the world did we get here?"

It was a great question . . . one that needed to be answered. We decided to take a month away from the business. We packed up and headed to St. Augustine, Florida, for a spiritual cleansing. It was time to be honest about where we'd been, what we were doing, and where we were going as a family. It was 2014.

I spent a lot of time during our sabbatical thinking about my faith. I realized I had always been a "half in, half out" Christian. I wanted to be completely sold out to God, but I was afraid to go all the way. I kept one foot in the world of success, accolades, and wealth accumulation so I'd have something to fall back on if God didn't come through like I hoped He would. I was glad to preach, go on mission trips, and serve in any capacity . . . as long as it didn't interfere too much with my business and family goals.

We took time off because I sensed God leading me to leave the chaos and pressure of New Jersey. After we got back and into the grind again, I believed He wanted me to step away from the business world and serve Him with all my heart. By the following year, we had made all the arrangements and moved to Florida. Our denomination didn't have a church in the area, so I made a commitment to start a Bible study in our home with the hope that it might someday grow to become a church. Soon after we arrived, a church in Flagler Beach, just south of St. Augustine, called me. Their pastor had a moral failure, and they had heard I was planning to launch a Bible study. The chairman of their board asked, "Would you come down and teach for us every Sunday until we find a new pastor? We don't have a teaching elder, and we think you'd be perfect in the interim."

I talked to Sung, and we decided to accept the invitation to teach. My first Sunday was Easter of that year. I guess it went pretty well because the board asked me to be the interim pastor for the next year. That would give them some breathing room to find a permanent replacement. I was ambivalent about the decision, but I decided to say "yes." I began commuting thirty miles to the church, and I quickly discovered that I'd had no idea what kind of load a pastor shoulders. I thought they spent their time preparing sermons, hugging people, and playing golf, but I was soon immersed in a myriad of difficult decisions—and sometimes tense relationships—that are the heart of pastoring a church . . . and are the biggest reasons pastors burn out.

My vision is always to reach out to people who feel overlooked . . . like I'd been for so long. The church was only a block from the beach, and I thought it was obvious that God wanted us to connect with the surfers, the beach bums, and the people in the community who lived on the margins. That's what Jesus did, and that's what we were going to do. What could possibly go wrong?

The answer is: A lot! I violated one of the cardinal rules of leadership, especially leadership in the church. I didn't ask enough questions, and I didn't listen to the concerns and hopes of the people in the church. I completely missed their hearts. Many of the people in the church were retired, and they loved their close-knit relationships. In addition, they were reeling from the trauma of having to deal with their trusted pastor betraying his calling, leaving a vacuum in one sense, but leaving broken hearts, too. People were confused, angry, hurt, and afraid. When I waltzed in with a grand plan to reach the down-and-out, the people in the church felt I had overlooked their wounds and fears. And they felt that way because I had. I blew it.

The problem was compounded because I was oblivious to my mistake. I raised money to build a café for youth group activities and to attract people from the beach and the town. Finally, the board chairman met with me and said bluntly, "Michael, it's great that you have a heart to reach people and pour your energy and time into that work, but that's not where we are. We need to change directions." We had a very frank conversation about the direction of the church, and it became apparent that I wasn't the right person for the permanent position of pastor. I had hoped it would work out that way, but my hope was dashed that day. I affirmed my commitment to stay for the rest of the year, but after that, I was done.

As my last Sundays approached, the board and many people of the church were very kind and affirming, but I was angry with God. I'd taken the job for a year with high expectations of leading a lot of people to Christ and building a church of loving, wise, generous members. Instead, I spent a lot of my time managing conflicts and trying to keep the sheep from biting each other! I wasn't always successful. Quite often, one of the guys on our staff team wasn't happy when I invited new people to join the worship team, and he wasn't shy about expressing his disapproval or giving feedback. On many Sunday mornings before I stepped onto the stage to preach, he would confront me and share his unhappiness with what we were doing with the worship team. I had prepared to share the love of Jesus with the people those mornings, but I felt like punching that guy in the nose! Why was God letting so many things like this happen when all I wanted to do was lead the church in knowing Jesus better?

After that debacle, our family started attending a church in St. Augustine, but I didn't tell Sung or anyone else about my seething anger. I just bottled it up, and I tried to numb my feelings with alcohol. A few years earlier, I had been introduced to Jiu Jitsu, which I instantly loved, so I tried to unwind through an exercise regimen. I was still wearing the mask of a secure, confident, self-assured man, but I was boiling inside. I hoped this new sport would help me let off some steam.

RADICAL HONESTY

The pressure, though, didn't subside. Finally, I knew I had to talk to Sung and lay it all out. The news didn't come as a surprise to her. She had seen very clearly that I was acting in ways to mask my intense resentment and discouragement. She was magnificent. Sung is a former Marine, but she has a tender heart. She told me, "I'm with you no matter what. You can tell me anything." And I did. She saw beneath the surface and assured me, "I know that personal commitments didn't mean much to you as you were growing up, but I'm in this with you for the long haul. Whatever hurt you're feeling, coping behaviors you've used, and masks you've been wearing, I'm not leaving."

I already knew Sung loved me, but this moment was incredibly powerful. This kind of love was something I'd never imagined. This kind of love was something I'd never known as a boy. This kind of love could reach down and heal the deepest hurts and forgive the biggest sins. Like Jesus, she knew the worst about me and loved me still. I had been terrified to tell her the truth, but her love invited me to be honest, and my honesty opened the door to more understanding, affection, and trust than I'd ever dreamed possible. Later, when we talked about this conversation, she told me, "God showed me what you were going to become, the finished work, the man that you'll become, and that has given me confidence that He wasn't through with you."

I had been terrified to tell her the truth, but her love invited me to be honest, and my honesty opened the door to more understanding, affection, and trust than I'd ever dreamed possible.

Not long after this breakthrough, two hurricanes, Matthew and Irma, devastated the Florida coast, including St. Augustine. Our house was severely damaged, so we had to move out until the repairs were completed. It was a kind of a Job story: my dreams of being a pastor had been shattered, our house was obliterated, and I'd sold the packaging business over a year before. At that point, I had no idea what God was going to do with me. During that time, I went to a spiritual retreat in Minneapolis. I'm not sure why I went because neither Sung nor I have any connections with Minnesota. While at the retreat, I met some wonderful believers, including Jay, who used to play professional football for the Vikings. He invited our family to come up for Thanksgiving, and he told us that Minnesota is a wonderful place to live. (It was hard to imagine a place that cold in the winter could trump the beaches of Florida, but we realized they don't have many hurricanes up there!) I have a friend who lives in Lakeville, a small town outside the city. When I called him and said we might consider moving there, he instantly told me, "That's great! You can plug into our church."

Always up for an adventure, Sung and I decided to make the move, and we found a house in the community called The Spirit of Brandtjen, an old farm that became a housing development. When we went to the church, Sung met a lady named Michelle and her husband Dave. A few minutes later, Sung ran up to me and exclaimed, "Michael, I found you a dad!"

That wasn't the kind of statement she'd ever uttered before, and I was more than a little confused. I rolled my eyes and replied, "I didn't know I was looking for a dad." She looked disappointed, so I said, "Sounds promising. Can't wait to meet him." But of course, I hoped that was the end of that discussion. She was well aware that I still had a hole in my heart created by the dysfunctional relationship with my father, and in fact, I'd recently learned that he wasn't my biological father at all. My mother had an affair with a married man which resulted in her getting pregnant, and instead of having an abortion, she let my dad think I was his child. I had faced years of pain from someone who wasn't even related to me!

The next Sunday, I met Dave, and Sung was right: he became my spiritual father, mentor, and dear friend. He has four daughters, and I was the son he never had. From the beginning, I saw that Dave was a passionate adherent of radical honesty. He told me about the arguments he had with Michelle, and how they resolved them and reaffirmed their love. That was foreign to me. When I was a kid, every argument was followed by verbal and sometimes physical battering, threats of divorce, and even deeper, unhealed wounds. In my family, divorce was the solution of choice. All but one couple in my extended family have been divorced: aunts, uncles, parents, and grandparents. That's a primary reason I had been afraid to be honest with Sung. If we argued, I assumed we were going to get divorced. Dave's honesty and commitment to Michelle shattered my false (but very powerful) assumptions. He modeled what it means to be a transparent, courageously honest Christian husband and father.

By that time, I'd been a Christian for fourteen years, but I was still living in a self-imposed prison. Jesus had set me free, but I hadn't walked out of the cell.

For me to live in freedom, God needed to give me a wonderfully patient and loving wife and a father figure who spoke with a beautiful blend of grace and truth. Dave loved me enough to tell me what I needed to hear. Since I'd been in the Navy, I'd projected an image of a composed, totally secure, supremely confident man. People were very reluctant to confront me, and that's exactly the way I wanted it. Dave knew that was only a game I played to keep people from seeing the hurt, insecurity, and fear that plagued my thoughts, and he patiently helped me embrace honesty instead of living a lie. Dave didn't need me, he didn't depend on me for a position or a salary, he wasn't impressed with all of my accomplishments, and he wasn't fooled by my bravado. He just loved me for who I am, and he wanted me to live in truth. He still does.

One of the most important conversations I had with Dave was when he told me to stop blaming my father for all my problems. Yes, there was abuse. Yes, I was damaged, and my dad was responsible for his actions, but it was time for me to be responsible for my healing and growth. He told me I had a choice: to continue to use my dad's behavior as an excuse for all of my acting out . . . or man up, be honest with God, him, and Sung, and trust God to use the broken parts of my heart to build something new, strong, and beautiful.

He told me I had a choice: to continue to use my dad's behavior as an excuse for all of my acting out . . . or man up, be honest with God, him, and Sung, and trust God to use the broken parts of my heart to build something new, strong, and beautiful.

I'd read the Bible voraciously since I'd trusted in Christ, but suddenly, I saw passages that described the benefits of being honest, as well as the cost of dishonesty. In the opening chapters of Genesis, Adam and Eve disobeyed God and ate from the forbidden tree. When God confronted them, Adam blamed Eve, and then he blamed God for giving Eve to him. And Eve blamed the serpent for her sin. And what was their sin? The serpent promised that if they ate the fruit, they'd "be like God"—independent, self-controlled, and answering to no one. Isn't that at the heart of all of our sins, too?

The Proverbs have a lot to say about honesty and deceit. For instance: "Better is a poor person who walks in his integrity than one who is crooked in speech and is a fool" (Proverbs 19:1). In other words, in God's eyes, honesty is far more valuable than riches gained by deceit. And as I can attest, living a lie makes us always fearful that someone will look behind the curtain and see the truth about us. King Solomon wrote, "Whoever walks in integrity walks securely, but he who makes his ways crooked will be found out" (Proverbs 10:9).

We may think we can fool people, and we may succeed for a long time, but sooner or later, we'll stand before God to give an account. Even now, God's Word is a knife to cut into our hearts and a light to shine on whatever is there. The book of Hebrews was written to believers who were being persecuted for their faith. The writer reminded them that God is always looking behind the curtain: "For the word of God is living and active, sharper than any two-edged sword, piercing to the division of soul and of spirit, of joints and of marrow, and discerning the thoughts and intentions of the heart. And no creature is hidden from his sight, but all are naked and exposed to the eyes of him to whom we must give account" (Hebrews 4:12-13).

Is it normal for men, even Christian men, to be committed to honesty? No, I don't think so. In fact, I think it takes uncommon courage. Many of us have desperately tried to hide our sins, lusts, addictions, and wounds for decades. It's exhausting, and it robs us of peace and meaningful relationships. It's time for a change.

During that season of my life, someone gave me a book called *Extreme Ownership*, written by Jocko Willink and Leif Babin, former Navy SEALs. From the first page, I was captivated by their story of fighting in Fallujah during the most intense part of the Iraq War. They write, "The book derives its title from the underlying principle—the mind-set—that provides the foundation for all the rest: Extreme Ownership. Leaders must own everything in their world. There is no one else to blame." As SEAL team leaders, Willink and Babin learned the value of being completely, utterly responsible for every decision. Jocko explains, "I had to take complete ownership of what went wrong. That is what a leader does—even if it means getting fired. If anyone was to be blamed and fired for what happened, let it be me."[3]

Jocko Willink exemplifies radical honesty and challenged me to "take complete ownership" of every aspect of my life—the wonderful, the horrible, the joys, the grind, and the secrets. And Dave modeled what it means to be a man of God who is committed to live in truth during every moment and every relationship. Because of them, I'll never be the same.

THINK ABOUT IT:

1. What's so appealing about "image management"? How does it work?

2. What are the costs we pay for wearing masks and trying to deceive ourselves and others—internally in our thoughts and assumptions and externally in our behavior and relationships?

3. As you've watched people over the years, what are some of the most common "masks" men wear?

4. Look again at Hebrews 4:12-13. Is "radical honesty" attractive or scary to you? Explain your answer.

5. Who is the most authentic man you know? Describe his impact on others, including you.

6. Do you think it's easier or harder for men who are Christians to be radically honest? If it's harder, explain the internal and external dynamics that keep men dishonest.

7. What difference does it make that God knows the very worst about you and loves you still? Do you have someone in your life who loves you like that? If so, what's the result for you? If not, where can you find that person?

CHAPTER 3

The Fearless

Fear not, for I am with you;
    be not dismayed, for I am your God;
I will strengthen you, I will help you,
    I will uphold you with my righteous right hand.

—Isaiah 41:10

> Life is not a journey to the grave with the intention of arriving safely in a pretty and preserved body, but rather to skid in broadside, thoroughly used up, totally worn out, and loudly proclaiming, "Wow . . . what a ride."
>
> —Adam Brown

Shortly after moving to Minnesota, Sung and I got involved at River Valley Church just outside of Minneapolis, and we loved it there. I began attending an in-depth discipleship course, and one of the lessons was on our identity in Christ. The truths surrounding this concept form the bedrock of our security and propel our motivations. I already knew these truths prior to joining this study. Heck, I could have taught them, but for me they were only intellectual knowledge. They hadn't yet penetrated my powerful defenses and melted my heart. God picked this time to drill down to the core of my pride and fear. It was painful, it was ugly, and it was absolutely necessary.

My friend, Dr. Ron Eccles, invited Sung and me to join him at a Christian conference in Tampa designed for business owners and their spouses. He called it "Roar," like a lion's roar. There were a couple of dozen people there. Ron is a brilliant executive coach, and I looked forward to learning more from him, but we almost didn't go. Our daughter Tehya, who was thirteen years old at the time, was neck deep in teenage drama, and we didn't want to leave while things were unsettled. Dave and Michelle assured us that they would step in during the days we were away, so we left for Tampa with high expectations (and a measure of anxiety about leaving Tehya).

We arrived at the hotel late at night before the first day of the event. When I got out of the rental car, I noticed a strip club next door. I wasn't tempted to go, but I wondered why a man who is as sharp as Ron would host a meeting with business leaders next to a place like that. It was just the first of a series of odd occurrences.

We were exhausted from a hectic week of work and all the family drama, and we were looking forward to a good night's sleep. When we got to our hotel room door, the key didn't work. I tried everything I knew to do, but we had to go back down to the lobby and ask for another key. This time, we got into the room and threw our bags on the bed. Sung went into the bathroom to get ready for bed, and in a minute or two, she came out to tell me, "Michael, the toilet is backed up." I called maintenance to get someone to fix the toilet, but the guy said he didn't have a plunger. I wanted to shout, "You've got to be kidding!" But I just asked when it would be fixed. He said we'd have to wait until the next morning.

Great. Just great.

The storm clouds in our room vanished the next morning. The toilet was unplugged, and I went for a long run while Sung was getting ready. After breakfast, Ron led us in an outstanding session. We felt understood, affirmed, and challenged. Business leaders in the room shared their struggles and victories. It was exactly why we had come, but I had an unsettled feeling. In fact, I felt intimidated by the sheer power and wisdom of the other people in the room. I wasn't sure why God had us there, but I was confident there was, in fact, a good reason.

As we walked toward the room where we were having lunch, I felt a strong urge from the Lord to skip lunch and go for a run. I protested, "God, that doesn't make any sense. I ran this morning, and I'm here now with Sung and the others. I'm going to stay right here." I sensed the Lord say, "I just want to spend time with you." I tried to ignore the "still, small voice," but the urge persisted, so I hesitantly told Sung, "Hey, I know this sounds odd, but I think the Lord wants me to go for another run to spend some time with Him. If you can save me something to eat, that would be great." She has lived with me long enough to know that I sometimes do things that are, to say the least, unconventional. She smiled, and I headed to our room to change clothes.

When I got down to the front desk, I asked the clerk, "Which way is the beach?"

He told me, "You're not far. Go down to the second intersection, take a left, go three blocks, and you're there."

"Great. Thanks!" I hit the pavement. I don't know if I followed his directions or not, but suddenly I had a déjà vu: I recognized a hotel where I'd stayed on a business trip in 2013, just after my dad passed away. The stress at the time had gotten to me. After my meetings, I spent two days drinking and drugging. I didn't want to feel anything. Over those two days, when the liquor stores were closed and I needed something, I got directions to a little house down a street near the hotel. A seventy-year-old lady who introduced herself as Miss Mary sold alcohol and drugs out of her living room—she literally had what I can only describe as a mini-pharmacy that she operated in this little urban house in downtown Tampa. While I used Mary's products, I spent hours both nights talking to her about everything imaginable . . . even God.

As these memories flooded my mind, my heart was pounding. I sense God leading me down the street to the house. I wanted to forget all of this again, but I knew it was something God was serious about. I jogged down the street past the houses in the recently revitalized development until I got to the one I recognized as Miss Mary's. I stopped. Out of breath and a bit anxious, I looked at the street sign—the street was named "Grace." I fell to my knees and started crying.

He took me there to remind me that even in one of my darkest nights, His grace was still shining brightly.

This moment was a remarkable breakthrough. God had led me back to a place of my deepest despair and worst brokenness—but not to condemn me. He took me there to remind me that even in one of my darkest nights, His grace was still shining brightly.

I ran back to the hotel, but the whole way I was bawling. I'm sure people stared at me and wondered what in the world was happening, but I couldn't stop crying. I went to our room, took a shower, and changed clothes, but when I looked in the mirror, my eyes were as puffy and red as a losing boxer's.

I went down to the room where the next session was about to start. When Sung saw me, she asked the obvious question, "What happened to you?"

"I don't know if I can tell you the whole story . . . certainly not here and certainly not now. I'll tell you later."

That wasn't a good enough answer, so she pulled me aside and insisted that I tell her what was going on. As I shared the story, strangely, she was smiling. She said, "That's so awesome that God showed you that!" I was having a hard time processing what had just happened down the street, but Sung intuitively understood that God was doing something powerful in my life.

We sat down for the afternoon session with Ron, and I had a sense that God wanted me to share it with everybody there. I wanted to tell God, "You've got to be kidding! I was already intimidated by these guys, and now You want me to tell them about the lowest point in my life? I'm already ashamed. Do You want me to be utterly humiliated?" But I waited to see if the sense of God's leading continued. It did. I leaned over and whispered, " Honey, I think God wants me to share what just happened."

She smiled and told me, "I'd listen to God."

As Ron began, he asked, "Before we start this afternoon, did any of you have a breakthrough this morning? Has God been speaking to you? We have some time for you to tell us if you will."

I haltingly raised my hand as I prayed, "Lord, I'm going to trust You right now." And I shared the story just as I've written it in this chapter, but I added an important part that came to me as I talked. One of the nights I was in the hotel—after a night of partying and my failure to show up at my scheduled business appointment the next morning—Sung called the hotel to find me because I hadn't called her the night before. When she couldn't reach me, she called the hotel operator. The hotel clerk came to my room and told me to call her, and when I got her on the phone, I lied. I told her I'd overslept, left my cell phone in my rental car and only recently retrieved it.

When I finished telling the story to the group, I concluded, "That's what happened at lunch. That's why I wasn't with Sung during the meal."

I sat down, exhausted but relieved that I had done what God told me to do. Instantly, three people raised their hands. A lady said, "I have the same story. Ten years ago I locked myself in a room in this hotel. I was drunk out of my mind. I'm so glad I don't have to keep this a secret any longer."

Another guy told us, "I just got out of my third rehab clinic for cocaine addiction. This is the first time I've told anyone outside my immediate family and my mentors."

Another man shared, "I lied to my wife every time I took a business trip. I can finally come clean."

Ron took a deep breath and told us, "This is remarkable. I've never seen people so open with each other so quickly. Thank you, each of you, for your courage to be honest with us."

WHO DETERMINES WHO WE ARE?

Our sense of who we are is shaped by many different factors. Children are like sponges, soaking up the verbal and nonverbal

messages in their environment. Those messages become the soft-
ware that runs our hearts and minds. If we've internalized messages that we're cherished by our parents, we're much more likely
to develop a deep sense of security and personal value. We'll
believe we're treasured because we've been treasured.

Sadly, that's not the experience for many of us. Our homes,
even the best of them, usually have several radios blaring disso-
nant messages to us: we're loved, but only when we perform up
to our parents' standards; we're safe, but only if we don't mention
certain topics; when we mess up, we have to earn our way back
into our parents' good graces; we're objects whose value is only to
please our parents, and if we don't, we're in big trouble. All of us
carry the baggage of being fallen people who live in a fallen world,
and for some of us, a fallen world includes abuse, abandonment,
and addiction. We carry the scars—and maybe the unhealed
gaping wounds—of a painful past. What we believe about ourselves, the world, and God becomes self-fulfilling: If we believe
we're unworthy of anyone's love, we can't feel the warmth of love
even when it's genuine. And if we've internalized messages that
we aren't safe, we may lash out in anger at any perceived threat,
we may run from anyone who is more powerful and therefore
threatening, or we may do anything and everything to please that
person to dampen the anger.

For me, the voice of my ninth-grade math teacher and my
dad's verbal abuse played on a continuous loop in my head for
decades. Maybe you can relate. Some of the voices on our tapes
might sound like one or more of these:

- "I'll never let anybody hurt me again."
- "I can't afford to be wrong, or people will make fun of
  me."

- "I'm worthless."
- "I'm unloved . . . and worse, I'm unlovable."
- "I can't let anybody know what I'm really thinking and feeling."
- "If I can't win, I won't play."
- "I can't stand it if anybody is upset with me."
- "I'm not as smart as . . . , not as handsome as . . . , not as talented as . . ."

When we're winning the performance game and we're looking pretty good, we feel superior to those who aren't cutting it. But when we fail, or when anyone sees that we're not what we claim to be, we lapse into rage or self-pity . . . or if we're really messed up, both! Nobody wins at this game. Even when it appears that we've got it all together, we're self-absorbed, using people for our gain instead of really loving them—and sooner or later, we'll be running on empty.

To a great degree, others have determined who we are—they shape our perceptions of ourselves. But the Bible tells us that when we come to Christ, God determines our identity. As our Savior, He bought us, and as our King, He rules over us in love.

At the moment of our salvation, a "great exchange" takes place. All of our sins are put on Christ, and His sacrifice on the cross is the just payment for all of them—past, present, and future. We're completely forgiven. That's incredible, but that's not all. Jesus' righteous life was credited to our account, so when God looks at us, He sees people who are totally forgiven and declared righteous in His sight. Jesus gets our sins, and we get His righteousness.

Paul expressed the exchange in two important passages. In his second letter to the Corinthians, he wrote, "For our sake

[God] made [Christ] to be sin who knew no sin, so that in him we might become the righteousness of God" (2 Corinthians 5:21). In his letter to the Philippians, he explained that the status, wealth, and honor he had as a highly respected Pharisee didn't compare to the wonder of being forgiven and declared righteous: "But whatever gain I had, I counted as loss for the sake of Christ. Indeed, I count everything as loss because of the surpassing worth of knowing Christ Jesus my Lord. For his sake I have suffered the loss of all things and count them as rubbish, in order that I may gain Christ and be found in him, not having a righteousness of my own that comes from the law, but that which comes through faith in Christ, the righteousness from God that depends on faith" (Philippians 3:7-9).

We find other amazing contrasts in Paul's letter to the Ephesians. We were dead, but we've been made alive in Christ. We were under the domination of the evil one, but now we belong to God. We were outcasts and foreigners to the grace of God, but Jesus has brought us into God's family (Ephesians 2:1-5, 11-22).

Peter needed to understand grace as the basis of a restored relationship with Jesus (as we'll see later in this chapter). In his first letter, he declared our identity in glowing terms: "But you are a chosen race, a royal priesthood, a holy nation, a people for his own possession, that you may proclaim the excellencies of him who called you out of darkness into his marvelous light. Once you were not a people, but now you are God's people; once you had not received mercy, but now you have received mercy" (1 Peter 2:9-10).

In ancient Israel, the most important positions were king and priest, and Peter makes the astounding claim that because of

Christ, you and I are members of a "royal priesthood," combining the two roles. Our standing with God isn't based on our ability to earn points and impress Him; it's entirely by His incredible grace. Jewish people reading this passage in Peter's letter would instantly recognize the language. Just before God gave Moses the Ten Commandments, God told him to tell the people, "Now therefore, if you will indeed obey my voice and keep my covenant, you shall be my treasured possession among all peoples, for all the earth is mine; and you shall be to me a kingdom of priests and a holy nation" (Exodus 19:5-6). "His own possession" in Peter's letter is the same as "treasure" in Exodus. Get this: God considers you and me to be His treasure! God considers himself rich because He has you and me! (Ephesians 1:18)

If we pay attention when we read Paul's letters, we see that our identity is inextricably tied to Jesus:

- We died with Him (Galatians 2:20).
- We were buried with Him (Romans 6:4).
- We were raised with Him (Colossians 3:1).
- We are seated with Him on the throne at the right hand of God (Ephesians 2:6).
- We were made alive with Him (Colossians 2:13).
- We are hidden with Him (Colossians 3:3).
- We are co-heirs with Him (Romans 8:17).

How did all this happen? It's always and entirely by God's amazing grace. Some people have a limited concept of grace. Nothing in this life is a free gift, so they assume grace isn't really free either. They may go to church and Bible studies, sing the songs, read their Bibles, and pray, but at the core of their hearts, they still believe they have to earn God's love and acceptance. They've lived their lives trying their best to be decent and competent—which is a good thing, by the way—but they trust more in their decency and competence than in Jesus. They don't really believe they were lost but then found, wretches with no hope who were cleansed with the blood of God's own Son and given a new status as a child of God. So they miss out on the wonder of knowing the love that surpasses knowledge.

It's the greatest display of unvarnished love in the history of the universe, and it's a free gift to everyone who is humble enough to take it. Grace rivets our attention on Jesus.

Our only hope was for a perfect Savior to take our place and pay for our sins. It's the greatest display of unvarnished love in the history of the universe, and it's a free gift to everyone who is humble enough to take it. Grace rivets our attention on Jesus. Who are we that He would give himself for us? The Creator humbled himself to become the Suffering Servant and our Savior. Sixteen centuries ago, Augustine described the wonder of it all:

> Man's maker was made man that He, Ruler of the stars, might nurse at his mother's breast; that the Bread might hunger, the Fountain thirst, the Light sleep, the Way be

tired on his journey; that the Truth might be accused of false witness, the Teacher be beaten with whips, the Foundation be suspended on wood; that Strength might grow weak; that the Healer might be wounded; that Life might die.[4]

In a recent discipleship study I attended, the author of our study guide stepped back to give us a better view of the meaning of Christ's sacrifice:

> As horrible as the crucifixion was from a human standpoint, the greatest agonies of the cross are not what the Roman soldiers did to Jesus, but what God did to Jesus. There was a spiritual side to the cross, and it was that spiritual side that caused Jesus to fall on the ground in Gethsemane [the night before He was killed] and ask God to let this cup pass from Him.
>
> It is the great exchange. He became sin for us and we became the righteousness of God in Christ. He became as we were so we could become as He is. He became sin, sickness, forsaken, weak, poor, and wretched so we could be righteous, healed, accepted, strong, rich, and dearly loved. He did what He did so we could be free.[5]

Do you really believe this? Don't answer too quickly. Everything in us would rather earn love and security instead of receiving it as a gift. Don't believe me? Look around at all the people who call themselves Christians who live graceless lives—and for many years, one of those people was me! Through a long, hard process, I've realized that I'm not the *hero* of my story. Jesus is.

I'm not the *author* of my story. Jesus is. I'm not the one behind the curtain *pulling strings* to make things happen. Jesus is. When I was the hero, author, and string puller, I made sure I told people the impressive parts about my career in the Navy, training to be a SEAL, and my success in business, but I left out the ugly parts. I was radically committed to image management, not Jesus.

God has put people like Dave into my life to help me separate *what I do* from *who I am*. The two overlap, of course, but for far too long, my identity was completely determined by two things: the trauma I experienced in my home when I was a child and the successes I enjoyed in the service, in business, and my college degrees. My primary goal was to impress people. To be honest, I didn't know there was any other way to live. Gradually, Dave imparted the truth that God is the only true source of love, security, confidence, and hope. Before, no matter how much I achieved, I was always afraid I'd fail the next time out or someone would be more successful than me. With my new identity as a loved, forgiven, accepted child of God, I could finally be what I tried to project so long: FEARLESS.

The Bible contains a lot of references to warfare—not just the battles to conquer the Promised Land in the Old Testament, but our fight now with the world (the promises that success, pleasure, and approval will give us the fulfillment we long for), the flesh (our inner compulsion to seek fulfillment outside of God), and the devil (whose strategy includes tempting us, deceiving us, and accusing us so we live in shame instead of freedom). Every morning, I have a choice: to fight *against* God by giving in to these forces, or to fight *with* and *for* God by choosing to honor Him and advance His kingdom on earth so it becomes a little more "as it is in heaven."

In our self-dependence, we often turn to ourselves to solve the problems of guilt and shame. We may try to ignore the problem, blame someone else, or make excuses, but even if we're born again, the nagging sense of shame takes root and poisons every desire and relationship. In his excellent book, *The Fight*, John White describes our flawed attempts to fix things, and he recommends a different solution:

> God's answer to your guilty conscience is the death of his Son. Your answer to a guilty conscience is usually something you do, like confessing harder, praying more, reading your Bible, paying more than your tithe in the offering and so on. These actions are what the writer to the Hebrews calls "dead works," the very things your conscience needs to be cleansed from and the very things that eventually get you wrapped up in the black shadow of your own guilt.
>
> Do you not understand? The Father does not welcome you because you have been trying hard, because you have made a thoroughgoing confession or because you have been making spiritual strides lately. He does not welcome you because you have something you can be proud about. He welcomes you because *his Son died for you.*[6]

We were born again into freedom by the grace of God, and we walk in freedom by the same grace. We live between "the already" and "the not yet"—we experience freedom, love, and power now, but these are, as Paul explains, just a down payment for all that will come in the new heavens and new earth. While we're in between, we still sin, we still mess up, we still hurt the people we love, and we still pursue our own kingdoms instead of God's. Denial, excuses, rationalizing, and blaming others are attempts to avoid culpability, but they don't work. But neither does self-hatred, self-flagellation, and groveling in shame long enough in a vain attempt to pay for what we've done. Self-pity is the opposite of the forgiveness, freedom, and joy Jesus has won for us on the cross! Don't go there. And if you're there, don't stay there.

When we align our hearts with God's, the battles we experience each day are categorically different. We're no longer obsessed with our power, our possessions, and our prestige. Instead, we care far more about trusting God to unleash His power to accomplish His purposes; we realize we're stewards—not owners—of everything God has put in our hands; and we care far more about Jesus' reputation than our own. In Jesus' most famous sermon, He explained that people usually spend their emotional energies on the wrong things, and then He redirects us: "But seek first the kingdom of God and his righteousness, and all these things will be added to you" (Matthew 6:33).

One time I was meditating on this verse during a period in our business cycle when I usually give sales goals to our staff. I wanted to apply the lesson Jesus was teaching, so this time I told our staff, "We're not going to have any lofty, challenging goals this year. We have a great team. I trust you to work hard, bring excellence to your job every day, and we'll live with the results." In case you haven't picked it up so far in this book, I'm a pretty disciplined and determined guy, so my staff team was stunned by my pronouncement. They were used to me asking them to pull off the impossible! A few months later, the pandemic hit, and hundreds of thousands of businesses went under. Instead of panicking, I sensed God tell me, "You're trusting Me and seeking My

kingdom, and I'm going to bless your business. You won't be lay-
ing people off. You'll be giving raises and bonuses this year."

I'd like to say that this assurance gave me perfect peace, but
that would be a lie. As I saw other business owners struggle, I
could easily imagine our company joining the list of those that
were closing their doors for good. In response to my anxious
thoughts, I told God again and again that I was going to trust Him
through it all. What happened? The year of the pandemic became
one of our best in the history of the company. I know that's not
the story of many faithful, godly business owners and employees,
but their story of God's provision may be just as amazing (and
maybe more so) than mine.

BROKEN . . . IN A GOOD WAY

The irony of the Christian life is that it's upside down from
the way the world works. To experience God's cleansing forgiveness, we have to admit that we sinned. To experience God's
power, we have to admit our weakness. To gain God's wisdom
and direction, we have to admit that we don't have all the answers.
If we admit that we've believed lies, we can hold on to God's truth.
To become fearless, we have to be honest about our fears. To be
whole, we have to admit that we're broken. To be qualified for the
kingdom of God, we have to admit that we're disqualified.

If there was ever a man who disqualified himself, it was Adam
Brown. His life had a storybook beginning in his hometown in
Arkansas: honor student, star on the football team, kind, respect-
ful, and happy. But a girlfriend badgered him to try cocaine, and
after one hit of crack, he was hooked. As an addict, he tried other
drugs, and one day in a drug-induced rage, he stabbed himself

in the neck. When the police arrived, they found him in a pool of blood, but he was alive. A quick check of his record revealed eleven felony drug and weapons charges—he was looking at a long stint in prison. At his hearing, the judge offered him a choice: prison or rehab. Brown chose rehab, and there, he heard the gospel of grace and trusted in Jesus. It was there that he met and fell in love with Kelley, also a committed follower of Christ. That's a beautiful story, but it's not the end of it.

Addiction doesn't give up easily, and after rehab, Brown continued to use. He wanted a complete change, so he talked to a Navy recruiter about becoming a pilot. The recruiter's background check also showed his long rap sheet and record of drug use. It looked like the end of a short road for Adam, but he contacted a friend whose father was the highest ranking Navy recruiter in the Southeast, and he got in. He had seen the *Navy SEALs* movie, and he wanted to become one. By this time, he was twenty-five years old, the oldest candidate to enter the training class in Coronado, California. About six months later, in April of 1999, he was one of a handful of graduates. In his biography of Adam's life, Eric Blehm remarks, "The training awakened in Adam the psycho who never quit. He also had Kelley and his faith, which gave him a refuge and a shield of strength." He was assigned to SEAL Team Four, deployed on the Southern U.S. border for counterdrug missions.

In 2003 a training accident damaged his right eye, so he learned to shoot lefthanded. He continued in combat support and intelligence in Iraq. A freak accident crushed and severed most of the fingers on his right hand, so he learned to shoot a pistol with his left hand. Finally, he reached his dream: he was assigned to SEAL Team Six, the most coveted and formidable group in the service, the top one percent of SEALs.

Adam's unit was assigned to the Kunar Valley in Afghanistan, then Iraq. One night, he and the team went on raids to destroy a terrorist network planting IEDs that had killed 70 percent of the coalition soldiers. His biographer comments, "This was one of the greatest victories in the war, executed almost entirely by two squadrons of DEVGRU SEALs, fewer than 100 men, killing more than 200 and capturing upward of 300. They saved thousands of lives." Adam received the Bronze Star for valor. The citation cites his "extraordinary guidance, zealous initiative and total dedication to duty."

Back in Kunar Valley, Adam distributed 500 pairs of shoes to impoverished kids. The dry atmosphere of the country gave his eye problems, so he flew home to have it removed. He had also broken a leg, and his ankles were in such bad shape that the doctor wondered how he could walk. While he was in the states, he earned an online bachelor's degree and made plans to apply to Harvard to earn an MBA when his tour was over.

When he returned to Afghanistan, Adam and the team received orders to take out a top-level Taliban leader. One night a helicopter dropped them into the area, and they got into a fierce firefight. They needed to get a grenade into the leader's hideout, but they were too far away. Adam ran to get closer, but was shot in the legs with an AK-47. On the ground, he drew fire from other fighters. He was carried out, but he died later at the base.

At his funeral in Arkansas, a SEAL who had been with him that night and knew him well told those who grieved his death: "Adam is the hardest man I have ever met. Over the course of his career he sustained more significant injuries than most of us combined, but he just kept on operating. He would not quit, he would not accept defeat. Not ever. Adam's devout Christian faith matched his toughness and fearlessness."[7]

Adam Brown's addiction had disqualified him from the future he wanted, but someone else, the ranking officer, stepped in to qualify him. That's what Jesus has done for us. In his letter to the Colossians, Paul encourages them to give "thanks to the Father, who has qualified you to share in the inheritance of the saints in light. He has delivered us from the domain of darkness and transferred us to the kingdom of his beloved Son, in whom we have redemption, the forgiveness of sins" (Colossians 1:12-14). What did it take to qualify us? It took the great exchange: "And you, who once were alienated and hostile in mind, doing evil deeds, [Jesus] has now reconciled in his body of flesh by his death, in order to present you holy and blameless and above reproach before him" (vv. 21-22).

The path to becoming fearless inevitably leads through the pain of being broken. As Christians, we're not immune to suffering. In fact, if we're serious about Jesus' invitation, "Follow me," we won't be surprised when He brings things into our lives (or allows them) that reveal our selfishness, and He calls us to something far bigger, far better, and far more meaningful. Author and spiritual mentor Henri Nouwen connects the dots for us:

> Jesus was broken at the cross. He lived his suffering and death not as an evil to avoid at all costs but as a mission to embrace. We too are broken. We live with broken bodies, broken hearts, broken minds, or broken spirits. We suffer from broken relationships.
>
> How can we live our brokenness? Jesus invites us to embrace our brokenness as he embraced the cross and live it as part of our mission. He asks us not to reject our

brokenness as a curse from God that reminds us of our sinfulness but to accept it and put it under God's blessing for our purification and sanctification. Thus, our brokenness can become a gateway to new life.[8]

Jesus isn't asking you and me to do anything He hasn't already done—to the nth degree. This kind of brokenness isn't like depression or despair that offer no hope, no light, no future. This kind is excruciating at first, but it results in more love and joy than we've ever imagined. It opens the door to an identity based on God's character, God's promises, and God's presence. Isn't that what you want? I sure do.

> This kind of brokenness isn't like depression or despair that offer no hope, no light, no future.
> This kind is excruciating at first, but it results in more love and joy than we've ever imagined.

One of the most poignant examples of restoration in the Bible is the scene on the shore at the end of John's Gospel. If anyone claims to be the worst failure in the world, they need to have a talk with Peter. At the Last Supper, he made a bold promise that he wouldn't forsake Jesus, no matter what, but Jesus told him he would deny Him three times before a rooster crowed. Only hours later, Jesus was arrested and faced a kangaroo court. Peter was waiting outside. He became nervous and scared when a servant girl recognized that he was one of Jesus' followers as they warmed themselves next to a charcoal fire. Later, two others asked if he was one of the disciples. After his third denial, the cock crowed, Jesus looked at Peter, and the fisherman "wept bitterly" in shame. For him, the dream seemed to be over.

But it wasn't.

Crushed by his shame, Peter, it appears, gave up on being part of the kingdom of God, so he went back to what he knew best: fishing. He took some other disciples with him, and they fished all night. As dawn broke, their nets were still empty, but they saw a man standing on the beach. He told them to throw their nets on the other side of the boat, and they hauled in a huge catch of big fish. They realized it was Jesus! When they got to shore, Jesus had already prepared breakfast for them over a charcoal fire. I don't think it was a coincidence that the smell of the fire reminded Peter of his greatest sin. Jesus took him aside and asked him three times, "Do you love Me?" By the third answer, Peter undoubtedly connected the dots. Jesus didn't gloss over Peter's sins, and He didn't excuse them or minimize them. He brought Peter face to face with them, and He forgave and restored him.

I believe this is what Jesus wants to do in each of our lives: remind us of our biggest sins and then forgive and restore us. That's the source of Peter's incredible courage for the rest of his life, and it's the source of our courage, too.

THINK ABOUT IT:

1. When we meet people for the first time, how do they generally identify themselves? What might this say about who or what defines them?

2. In what ways does trusting in our performance—our power, prestige, and possessions—make us insecure, feeling false superiority when we're doing well and real inferiority when we're not?

3. Look back at the "with Him" gospel statements in the chapter. What difference would it (or does it) make to really believe these truths?

4. To what extent are you aware of the fight with the world, the flesh, and the devil? Where do you see those in your experience?

5. Are you infuriated, confused, or inspired when you realize that you can't earn God's love and acceptance—that it's a free gift? Be honest, and explain your answer.

6. How would you describe "the path of brokenness"? To what extent have you embraced it? What will it take for you to be fully committed to it? What difference would that make?

7. Read the account in John 21:1-19 of Peter's encounter with Jesus on the beach. What do you think was going on in Peter's mind and heart as he saw Jesus on the shore, smelled the charcoal fire, and was asked three times if he loved Jesus?

CHAPTER 4

The Courageous

And others are the ones sown among thorns. They are those who hear the word, but the cares of the world and the deceitfulness of riches and the desires for other things enter in and choke the word, and it proves unfruitful.

—Mark 4:18-19

> A gladiator's first distraction is his last.
>
> —Oenomaus

I'll never forget the climactic scene in the movie *Braveheart* when Scotsman William Wallace rides back and forth in front of his soldiers and puts steel in their souls so they would fight for their independence against the king of England. The English army is in full view. When he rides up, he boldly announces, "I am William Wallace, and I see a whole army of my countrymen, here, in defiance of Tyranny. You've come to fight as free men, and free men you are. What will you do without freedom? Will you fight?"

Some in the ranks shout their unwillingness to fight. One speaks for many: "Fight? Against that? No! We will run! And we will live."

Then, Wallace gives one of the most iconic pronouncements: "Fight and you may die. Run, and you'll live . . . at least a while.

And dying in your beds, many years from now, would you be willing to trade all the days, from this day to that, for one chance—
just one chance—to come back here and tell our enemies that
they may take our lives, but they'll never take our freedom!"[9]

Wallace was using a "boast" to inspire his men. We usually
think of boasting as an expression of arrogance—and it usually is—but in the Bible, the term sometimes means something
very different. If it refers to people calling attention to their own
accomplishments, it's certainly pride, but if someone boasts in
God, it calls attention to His love, His power, and His glory. When
William Wallace called his soldiers to fight and die for freedom,
he was boasting in something much bigger than any individual:
their purpose to free their land from English oppression. The
Hebrew word *mahalal* means to praise or boast, and it's the root
of the word "hallelujah," which means "praise Jehovah." That's our
boast.

The biblical writers draw a clear distinction in the object of
boasts. We find the difference in a powerful passage when God
spoke through the prophet Jeremiah: "Thus says the Lord: 'Let
not the wise man boast in his wisdom, let not the mighty man
boast in his might, let not the rich man boast in his riches, but
let him who boasts boast in this, that he understands and knows
me, that I am the Lord who practices steadfast love, justice, and
righteousness in the earth. For in these things I delight, declares
the Lord'" (Jeremiah 9:23-24).

What do most people, including many Christians, pursue
with all their hearts? In other words, what's their boast? God puts
His finger on three of the most prominent: intelligence, power,
and wealth. He doesn't say those things are inherently wrong, but

it's certainly wrong when we make secondary things our primary thing. When that happens, we're more enamored with God's gifts than the Giver. God says there's something worth boasting in: understanding and knowing Him. But this doesn't lead to arrogance . . . just the opposite. We realize that God practices love, justice, and righteousness. Those three words require some unpacking.

What do most people, including many Christians, pursue with all their hearts? In other words, what's their boast? God puts His finger on three of the most prominent: intelligence, power, and wealth.

The *love* of God is *chesed*, covenant lovingkindness. This isn't superficial and changeable. It's God's rock-solid commitment to our good, and it never wavers or diminishes. We typically think of *justice* as punishment for wrongs committed, but in the Old Testament, it means that and something more: It includes justice for the poor expressed in sacrificial giving to meet their needs, kindness to the marginalized, and treating foreigners the way we treat people in our families. And *righteousness* doesn't just mean being honest and good. It means that, and much more. A righteous person disadvantages himself for the sake of others, but an unrighteous person disadvantages others for his own selfish aims. All of this sounds a lot like *grace*, doesn't it? And these aren't sterile, academic concepts. God says He *delights* in love, justice, and righteousness. In other words, He's thrilled when He displays those traits to undeserving people (like you and me), and He's thrilled when we treat others with that kind of love and generosity. God and His character are our boast. Nothing less and nothing else.

Except there's always something less and something else, isn't there? We're easily distracted, first to make small compromises, and then we justify larger ones. I envision myself on a highway with exits. Every *good thing* that's not a *God thing* is an exit. If I take one (I should say *when* I take one), I move away from God's heart and His purpose for me . . . just a little. But soon, that road has exits, and each of those take me even farther away. Pretty soon, it's easy to look up and wonder, *How'd I get here?* The answer is simple: we boasted in secondary things that sure seemed like the most important things at the moment of our decision.

Let me describe what the exits look like in my life.

PRESTIGE

After I left the Navy, I came back to the states, fell in love and married Sung, and God gave us the miracle of a baby. (Much more on that in the last chapter.) God was blessing me in ways that were mind-boggling, and my business was booming. I received a U.S. government contract that took me to thirty-three cities to make presentations regarding federal law as it relates to shipping hazardous materials. Each presentation was attended by thirty to seventy-five executives from several industries, including oil and

gas and pharmaceuticals. The schedule included three or four cities a week for ten weeks. When I signed the contract, I knew I was
going to sacrifice my time with Sung and the kids, but I wanted the
adrenaline rush of being the recognized expert standing in front
of industry leaders to give them what they couldn't get anywhere
else. Some of my colleagues sat in the audience, and they were
probably envious that the government had tapped me instead
of them for the job. Prestige, however, wasn't all that drove me.
I wanted the income into the company's bank account to prove
to our employees that I was a hard worker. But God showed me
there would be another sacrifice: my time with Him. I insisted
that I'd be faithful in my travels to spend time in the Word and
prayer, but I had a strong sense that He wasn't buying it.

In spite of my assurances to God, my witness quickly went
out the window. I went drinking with those who attended and
got involved in things that I'd been sure I'd steer clear of. When I
got on the plane after the thirty-third presentation, I was spiritually, physically, mentally, and emotionally spent . . . like a sponge
with all the water squeezed out. Those ten weeks were far more
destructive than I could have imagined. When I was a young
Christian, full of fire for the Lord, I looked at Christians who were
"backsliding" and shook my head. I claimed, "I'll never do that!
I'll never be that guy!" But I did . . . and I was. God had warned me
that this gig was an exit on my highway, and He was right.

The pursuit of prestige doesn't always end in getting what
we wanted. I got the accolades of being in front of the industry
executives and substantial income, and at a high price, but plenty
of people pay the price without achieving status. I remember
watching *Rambo* with my father, the Force RECON Marine. I'm

sure those moments with him, and my unfulfilled craving to be accepted by him, were at least part of the reason I wanted to be a SEAL. Those guys are superheroes, incredibly skilled and dedicated, the best of the best. And also, I wanted to prove that my ninth grade math teacher was dead wrong about me. I wanted to be a superhero, too.

Earlier I mentioned that in 1992, a team of SEAL recruiters came to Hawaii where I was stationed. I had seen the same Charlie Sheen *Navy Seals* movie that Adam Brown saw, and I was just as inspired by it. When I was a kid, my friends and I made swords from sticks and shields from cardboard. We played commando in the woods near the house, throwing rocks and even shooting our BB guns at each other. With my dad's military background, I was convinced intense warfare was in my DNA. When I met with the recruiters, one of them baited me. After describing the kind of missions they conduct, he sat back and offhandedly said, "But most people don't even make it through the first screening." It felt a lot like my math teacher was saying it, but this time, it was focused on a clear goal and a real passion. I wanted to bark back, "Oh yeah! I'll show you!" but I just asked for the application. The screening process takes about a year: filling out never-ending forms, getting approved by your CO, and passing a battery of psych evaluations and physicals. All of this was just to be able to show up at training with the chance to be tested to the limit and maybe, just maybe, become a SEAL. When I was approved, I had to sign up for four more years in the Navy. My course was set. I was locked and loaded.

I left Hawaii in August of 1994 and arrived in San Diego. I'd seen a movie, *The Finest Hour*, where, in the opening scene, the main character, played by Rob Lowe, drives over the Coronado Bridge to the training base.[10] When I drove over that bridge, I saw some sailboats underneath. At that moment, I vowed to complete training and my service, and then come back and live on a sailboat in Coronado Bay.

By the time I arrived for my BUD/S training, the Naval Special Warfare Center had implemented a four-week physical fitness program coined "fourth phase" that was meant to help reduce the attrition rate in the program. At the end, there were too many people qualified for the next phase, so they devised a physical fitness challenge. The ones who scored in the top half would be assigned to one class, and the rest would have to wait and be assigned to the following class. During the challenge, I fell on the obstacle course on the four-story tower dubbed the "Slide for Life." My tailbone hurt, but I got up and completed the cycle. I finished in the top half of the group, so I was in the next class. By that point, my tailbone *really* hurt, but I didn't tell anybody. I was going to tough it out because I was sure it would heal on its own. I didn't realize at the time that I had severely injured the bone.

As we started our class of SEAL training, we had a head-shaving party on the beach with pizza and beer, an initiation into the actual training program. I did well in the first part of training, but after that, my tailbone was really swollen and painful. Since I hadn't rested it to let it heal, the tissue around the broken bone got infected and swelled to the size of a grapefruit. I kept the pace in training, but I left blood stains wherever I sat. It looked like my rear end was bleeding . . . because it was! One day, I was doing sit-ups on the PT grinder under a sign that read, "The only easy day was yesterday." The tap-out bell was directly under the sign.

Men would ring it to signify they were dropping out because it was just too tough. As I did sit-ups, I tried to rock side to side so the pressure was on my butt cheeks and not my tailbone. I guess it looked a little odd because an instructor yelled at me, "Bowen, what's wrong with you?"

I didn't want to tell him what was really wrong, so I just yelled, "Hooyah!" the battle cry for SEAL trainees, and kept rocking. That wasn't good enough. He ordered me to run out to the beach and get covered in sand, and then keep doing sit-ups.

While I was gone, he looked at the PT grinder and saw blood where I'd been. He said, "Bowen, pull your pants down." When he saw the infected ball and the blood and a makeshift maxi pad, he shook his head and told me, "Man, this is bad. Go to the infirmary and have the doc take a look."

The doctor told me that my infection was severe and advanced, and I needed IV medication. I responded, "Just give me some medicine and let me get back out there. I'll get through it."

But he insisted, "No, it's too bad." Then he said what I dreaded to hear: "Bowen, you can't continue in the training."

I was devastated. My hopes were gone . . . my dream was shattered. As I sat in the Master Chief's office, I told him, "This is one of the worst moments of my life."

He tried to console me, "You'll have an opportunity to come back after you heal. We'll keep a place for you."

The Navy cut orders for me to report to Long Beach. I'd be joining the crew of a destroyer that was going to deploy to the Persian Gulf very soon after I arrived. I was again the Emergency Responder/Firefighter, but that job didn't compare to what I had dreamed of doing as a Navy SEAL. I felt lost, and there was nobody on the ship who could help me process all that had just happened. I dove into my work and was a stellar sailor. Again, I earned awards for my performance. I talked to the captain and asked, "When can I get back to SEAL training?" He assured me that it could happen after our deployment. That gave me some hope, but on the ship, there weren't many ways to stay in shape. A short time before, I had been in the best shape of my life (except for the busted tailbone), but I couldn't maintain my conditioning on board.

When we returned from deployment, I applied and was accepted into Surface Rescue/Swimmer training in San Diego to get in shape for the more rigorous physical demands I'd face in Coronado. Like me, several other guys in the program had been injured in SEAL training and were trying to get back there again. I was selected as the class leader—at the top of my game again. I was confident I was going to be accepted back into the training in Coronado, but soon after I completed Rescue/Swimmer training, I discovered that our ship was scheduled for another deployment. I talked to the Command Counselors about the prospects of getting back after this deployment, and they assured me they'd make that happen.

On this deployment, I was selected for the Visit, Board, Search and Seizure Team to board vessels suspected of carrying weapons of mass destruction. The training included firearms and ship boarding. This was as close as you can get to SEAL activities without actually being one of them. In fact, I later found out that SEAL teams were doing exactly the same thing we were doing.

Things were going great, and the Captain selected me for command advancement, making me an E-6, First Class Petty Officer. I quickly realized this was an honor I really didn't want.

I had become a valuable asset to the Captain and the ship, so it was going to be more difficult to transfer, and too, many of the instructors at SEAL training were E-5s and E-6s, so I would out-rank them. That could be a problem.

In spite of all my hopes to be a SEAL, it wasn't to be. While we were deployed, I received word that my father had a heart attack, and shortly after, I learned that my first wife was being charged with assault and our kids might be taken away. Instead of signing on for a career as a SEAL, I left the Navy and went home to take care of those problems.

Incredibly high goals—in any profession—can devastate those who don't reach them. In Basic Underwater Demolition/ SEAL training, about eighty percent of the most dedicated, talented, determined, and physically fit men don't pass. They remain in the Navy, but some simply can't cope with the death of their dream. In 2014, Danny DelBianco completed the obstacle course and other training elements before Hell Week. He had played rugby for the University of Southern California, and he was a stunning physical specimen. His father said Danny was "excited and very confident" he'd do well that week, but after fifty hours of the most rigorous drills and without sleep, Danny "tapped out" by ringing the bell, put his helmet with those of the other wash-outs, and walked back to the barracks for some sleep. Only hours later, he stepped off a ledge on the twenty-second floor of a hotel in San Diego.[11]

Few of us are looking for a career as demanding and elite as the SEALs, but the failure to earn our desired status can rock our worlds. We may become sullen for a short time and snap out of it, or we may become clinically depressed and require medical attention . . . or something in between. Relationships suffer as all the passion and drive is drained from our now empty emotional tanks, and we rocket between rage and self-pity.

Prestige is fine if we don't hold it too tightly. It can give us a platform to do amazing things for others. But if our grip on it is too tight . . . and its grip on us is too tight . . . we lose even when we win.

POWER

Prestige and power are connected, but they're not the same thing. Prestige is reputation; power is authority. A person can certainly have one without the other. In fact, some individuals wield enormous power behind the scenes, controlling people and situations while not having much of a public face. I advanced in the Navy and was in charge of people who were as much as fifteen years older than me. My position gave me authority, which carried both power and responsibility. Sadly, my dominant model of leadership had been my dad, so I assumed that authority meant leading with an iron fist. I always looked very sharp in my uniform, polished my insignia, and puffed my chest out.

When I got into the business world, I made sure people noticed the "Vice President" and then "President" titles on my business cards. These words were more than titles—they signified that I was someone to be reckoned with, a force of nature to be respected . . . if not feared.

We may try to exert power in our families to control our spouse and kids; in our work to control our boss, coworkers, and clients; in our church to force people to agree with us; and with God because we expect Him to jump through our hoops.

Power can be used for good, but when used inappropriately, it's not just wrong—it's extremely dangerous. When we insist on sitting on the throne, we push God off, and sooner or later, there's a reckoning. In *Gods at War*, Kyle Idleman explains:

> God declines to sit atop an organizational flowchart. He is the organization. He is not interested in being president of the board. He is the board. And life doesn't work until everyone else sitting around the table in the boardroom of your heart is fired. He is God, and there are no other applicants for that position. There are no partial gods, no honorary gods, no interim gods, no assistants to the regional gods. God is saying this not because he is insecure but because it's the way of truth in this universe, which is his creation. Only one God owns and operates it. Only one God designed it, and only one God knows how it works. He is the only God who can help us, direct us, satisfy us, save us.[12]

When we acknowledge God as the ultimate power over us, then and only then will we have the wisdom and humility to use the power vested in us to build people up instead of using them for our own goals.

POSSESSIONS

Prestige and power often are the means to financial gain, which gives us the capacity to acquire more and better stuff. Early in my professional career, I remember dreaming about, and then buying, a new Dodge Durango. Later, as business increased, I had enough money to buy Sung a BMW X5. We lived in New Jersey where several of my friends were executives in the financial markets . . . and they were rolling in the dough. They were Christians, and it seemed they had no qualms about spending a lot of money on luxuries. I quickly got into the not-so-subtle comparison contest. When one of them bought a bigger, nicer house, the rest of us felt pressure to upscale. When one of them went on a dream vacation, the rest of us started looking at packages in the Maldives or some other exotic place. When one of them had kids going to an expensive private school, the rest of us had to keep pace. I wasn't making the kind of money they made, so I couldn't keep up with them . . . but my heart was filled with the desire to! I wanted to own a mini-mansion in the finest neighborhood and keep up with my rich friends in every possible way. Comparison and competition were always in the background of my thinking, and often, those thoughts were blaring loud and long.

"Acquisition creep" happens in very small increments. We need a smart phone, and one we like costs a little bit more than we can afford, but we rationalize that we can use the extras it offers. We do the same thing with items in the grocery store, restaurants, technology, furniture, clothes, and everything else we buy. One upgrade isn't a big deal, but hundreds of them blow our budgets . . . and more significantly, they show that our hearts are more into things than into God. That was certainly true for me. I always looked for an upgrade—maybe because I thought I deserved it, maybe because I wanted to impress my friends, or maybe because my heart was fixed more on things than on God . . . or maybe it was all of those reasons.

Christians justify what we want and what we own by calling them God's blessings. To be sure, they may be, but when we think too much about our possessions, brag about our possessions, and fear losing our possessions, they own us instead of our owning them.

In the Christian world, there's another temptation: When we hear someone talk about how much they give to the church and other nonprofits—or worse, when we talk about how much we give—we're not following the directive to "give in secret" and receive the Father's reward. We need to hold prestige lightly, hold power lightly, and hold our possessions lightly. They just aren't that important! As Paul wrote to the Christians in Rome, "For the kingdom of God is not a matter of eating and drinking but of righteousness and peace and joy in the Holy Spirit" (Romans 14:17).

Years ago, a leading pastor was asked how we can tell if our hearts have wandered away from Christ. He answered that the best indicator is what we think about in our unhurried moments. In other words, what's foremost on our hearts bubbles up when we don't have to think about anything else. Is it Jesus' righteousness, the peace of God that comes from being forgiven and accepted, and the joy of sensing God's presence? Or is it our bank account, our next dream purchase, an honor or promotion we crave, or something else that's "passing away"? This exercise is challenging and sobering.

People with money are often powerful people, so others are hesitant to speak the truth to them about how they're using their money. No matter what our income level and bank balance might be, all of us need someone who has the guts to ask us hard questions about our relationship to money . . . and we need the guts to really listen. Jesus talked more about money than virtually any other subject. Why? Because the way we handle money is a window on our hearts.

PLEASURE

Entitlement. We live in the most comfortable culture the world has ever known, and many of us have concluded that we deserve pleasure, comfort, and ease. We love these things, we craft our lives so we have more of them, and we spend a lot of financial and emotional capital to get them. I'm in that boat, and I need to be careful to avoid the powerful temptations of pleasure. I work hard, so it's easy to assume that I deserve pleasure and entertainment, but when I demand it, I've crossed a line. How can I tell? By my attitude when I don't get it. Do I bluster or pout? Do I blame others or feel sorry for myself?

Again, there's nothing wrong with pleasure if it's God's gift. In fact, our greatest pleasure is the sheer joy of knowing God. In a beautiful psalm, David prayed, "You make known to me the path of life; in your presence there is fullness of joy; at your right hand are pleasures forevermore" (Psalm 16:11). And in another one, he writes that the power, riches, and pleasures he enjoys as a king don't compare to experiencing the love of God:

One thing have I asked of the Lord,
     that will I seek after:
that I may dwell in the house of the Lord

all the days of my life,
to gaze upon the beauty of the Lord
and to inquire in his temple. (Psalm 27:4)

If someone had access to every moment of my life for a week, what would they conclude is the "one thing" most precious to me? What do I consider so beautiful that I can't take my mind off it? For David, it was the Lord. As the king, I can imagine that he had plenty of distractions. I lead a company; he led a nation. And yet he was riveted on that one thing that was more precious than anything or anyone else.

REORIENTING OUR HEARTS

Centuries ago, Augustine identified our most fundamental problem as "disordered loves." It's not wrong to love prestige, power, possessions, and pleasure . . . unless we love them more than we love God. How can we tell what's most important to us? We can take a long hard look at our daydreams and longing. We can examine our worries and see what we're afraid of losing. Our most persistent and painful emotions—shame, hurt, fear, resentment, and anxiety—tell us what really matters to us.

In a commencement address at Kenyon College, novelist David Foster Wallace (who wasn't a Christian) compared our pursuit of secondary things to misplaced worship. He told the graduates:

If you worship money and things—if they are where you tap real meaning in life—then you will never have enough. Never feel you have enough. It's the truth.

Worship your own body and beauty and sexual allure and you will always feel ugly, and when time and age start showing, you will die a million deaths before they finally plant you. On one level, we all know this stuff already— it's been codified as myths, proverbs, clichés, bromides, epigrams, parables: the skeleton of every great story. The trick is keeping the truth up front in daily consciousness. Worship power—you will feel weak and afraid, and you will need ever more power over others to keep the fear at bay. Worship your intellect, being seen as smart—you will end up feeling stupid, a fraud, always on the verge of being found out.[13]

In his book, *Counterfeit Gods*, Tim Keller observes: "The only way to free ourselves from the destructive influence of counterfeit gods is to turn back to the true one, the living God. . . . he's the only one who if you find him, can truly fulfill you, and if you fail him, can truly forgive you."[14]

In Alcoholics Anonymous, the most difficult parts of the program are Steps 4 and 5 of the 12-step program. In Step 4, people are asked to take a "searching and fearless moral inventory" of their lives, to be ruthlessly honest, and in Step 5, they're asked to tell God and at least one other person what they uncovered in Step 4. This is the place where many people bail out of AA because they can't bring themselves to be completely honest with themselves or anyone else. This is the moment they've feared, so this is the moment of supreme courage.

It's the same for you and me. God is asking us to make a searching and fearless moral inventory of our distractions, the secondary things we've made primary, our counterfeit gods that have taken God's rightful place in our minds, hearts, and choices. And then, like I've done with some people I trust, God wants us to spill our guts, to lay it all out in the open—not so we'll be mocked and condemned, but so we can experience the wonder of grace, forgiveness, and the process of restoration.

God is asking us to make a searching and fearless moral inventory of our distractions, the secondary things we've made primary, our counterfeit gods that have taken God's rightful place in our minds, hearts, and choices.

Paul's letter to the Galatian believers is full of corrections. They had gotten off base and were no longer living by truth and grace. At the end, Paul wanted to drive a stake in their minds about what he considered the supreme value in his life. He told them, "But far be it from me to boast except in the cross of our Lord Jesus Christ, by which the world has been crucified to me, and I to the world" (Galatians 6:14).

What's your boast? What's mine?

THINK ABOUT IT:

1. As you imagine the road Christian men travel with Jesus in a life of love and purpose, what are the exit ramps for most men? What are your exit ramps?

2. What's the lure of prestige? What does it promise? Does it deliver? Explain your answer.

3. What's the lure of power? Who do you know who exercises authority with kindness? What impact does that person have on others, including you?

4. What's the lure of possessions? Describe how "acquisition creep" works. What do you have that you wasted your money on?

5. What's the lure of pleasure? How does a sense of entitlement shape our pursuit of pleasure?

6. Do you think David Foster Wallace overstated the case when he defined our longing for intelligence, beauty, wealth, and power as "worship"? Explain why or why not.

7. Look again at Galatians 6:14. What would it (or does it) look like in your life to boast only in the cross of Christ?

8. What is God saying to you through the concepts of this chapter?

CHAPTER 5

The Royal

The Spirit himself bears witness with our spirit that we
are children of God, and if children, then heirs—heirs of
God and fellow heirs with Christ.

—Romans 8:16-17

> I'm so thankful because of my relationship with Jesus
> Christ and being adopted in the family of God that I don't
> have to live the highs and the lows and the roller coaster
> that the rest of the world lives, because I know where
> my identity lies. My identity lies as a child of God, and
> that's something that will never be shaken.
>
> —Tim Tebow

Earlier I mentioned that my dad named me Michael Anthony after
two of his favorite characters in *The Godfather* movies. When I
was a little boy, he always called me "the king." I'm sure there was
some psychological projection that he really wanted to be seen as
a king, and he gave me that name as a substitute. Names seemed
to be more fluid with my dad than with other people. As I grew
up, I was sure my dad's name was Russell Anthony Bowen. His
nickname was Tony, and when he came home from Vietnam
and left the Marine Corps, he opened a bar called Tony's on the
Jersey shore. Not long before he died in 2012, my father trusted

in Christ, and those last weeks and months were wonderfully redemptive for our relationship. After he died, we received the death certificate: it read "Russell Max Bowen." No one ever knew his middle name was Max, not Anthony! For my entire life, I had assumed my middle name came from his, but that wasn't the case at all. I guess he loved *The Godfather* vibe so much that he named both of us after the characters!

After my mother told me that Dad wasn't my biological father, I had a DNA test to confirm her suspicion, and it did. Suddenly, a lot of assumptions were shattered, some more humorous than others. Dad had told me from early childhood that we were Italian (he probably should have said Sicilian to connect more closely with the Mafia), but my DNA shows not a drop of Italian ancestry. My mother had told me she was part Cherokee Indian, but there isn't a trace of Native American blood in me.

Dad was enamored with the Corleone family and its name, and he wanted the Bowen name to be revered—maybe not for the same reason, but still for the respect we would earn for our brilliance and power. Needless to say, it didn't quite work out that way. I've tried to change the narrative with my children. I tell them, "The way you act, the way you treat people, reflects on our family's name, but even more, it reflects on God because we bear His name as His children."

We can look at other royal families to see that some people honored their family name and others brought disgrace and shame. In England, Queen Victoria came to power when she was only eighteen as perhaps the least prepared sovereign in recent history, but she became one of the most successful. Under her sixty-three year rule, the empire expanded, the army and navy won many battles, and the economy flourished. Only a few decades after she died, her grandson Edward assumed the throne, but his love for an American divorcée created a crisis because the Church of England wouldn't allow a member of the royal family to marry a person who had been divorced. Edward tried to convince Parliament to grant him a waiver, but the Prime Minister refused. Edward's love for Wallis Simpson was greater than his love for the British Empire, so he abdicated the throne in 1936. Then, more recently, Prince Charles married a beautiful girl named Diana, but he had eyes (and other parts of his anatomy) for an ex, Camilla. The saga of Charles and Diana's strained and then failed marriage was set on the backdrop of Diana's winsome personality, stunning beauty, and passionate advocacy of human rights and social justice. In stark contrast, Charles came off like a cad.

As I write this chapter, the British royal family is in turmoil because Prince Harry and his wife, Meghan Markle, have moved to California. They couldn't handle the pressure of being under a microscope and living with the expectations of royalty, so they put aside at least some of their privileges to live free from the crucible of Buckingham Palace. News reports of tension in the family are, to say the least, credible.

As believers, our behavior as children of the King may not make the history books, but it matters . . . a lot.

IMPLANTED DNA

We sometimes use the term "child of God" kind of flippantly, but it's packed with meaning. To begin with, we most definitely weren't God's children before our sins were forgiven by the sacrifice of Christ, but now, we're His adopted sons. John's prologue says it beautifully: "The true light, which gives light to everyone, was coming into the world. He was in the world, and the world was made through him, yet the world did not know him. He came to his own, and his own people did not receive him. But to all who did receive him, who believed in his name, he gave the right to become children of God, who were born, not of blood nor of the will of the flesh nor of the will of man, but of God" (John 1:9-13).

It's helpful to look at two theological terms: *justification* and *adoption*. Justification, as you can gather from looking at the word, is a judicial verdict. We were in the courtroom, accused by Satan as sinners and standing guilty, deserving of God's just punishment. But Jesus stood in front of the bench and declared, "I'll take the punishment he deserves." And He did, on the cross. But justification has a second layer of meaning. As we saw earlier, we're not just forgiven, we're declared righteous. Christ's death is our substitute for the punishment we deserve, and His perfect life is our substitute for the righteous life we couldn't live. This dual truth about justification is magnificent, but it's not all.

In the courtroom, as the sentence of "not guilty" is declared, the judge has come down to adopt us into His own family! He becomes our Father. In his classic work, *Knowing God*, professor J. I. Packer writes:

> The free gift of acquittal and peace, won for us at the cost of Calvary, is wonderful enough, in all conscience— but justification does not of itself imply any intimate or deep relationship with God the judge. In idea, at any rate, you could have the reality of justification without any close fellowship with God resulting. But contrast this, now, with adoption. Adoption is a family idea, conceived

in terms of love, and viewing God as father. In adoption, God takes us into His family and fellowship, and establishes us as His children and heirs. Closeness, affection, and generosity are at the heart of the relationship. To be right with God the judge is a great thing, but to be loved and cared for by God the father is a greater.[15]

Why are so many Christian men lukewarm about their relationship with God? I'm convinced that at least one of the reasons is that they haven't yet been stunned by the fact that the Creator of the universe loves them dearly, delights in them, and has invited them to join Him in the family business of redeeming the world with, by, and for His Son.

As we begin to grasp the concept
of adoption, our hearts warm
to God, and every aspect of our
faith takes on a deeper, stronger
meaning.

As we begin to grasp the concept of adoption, our hearts warm to God, and every aspect of our faith takes on a deeper, stronger meaning. We read the Bible to understand His heart better. We pray to spend time with the one who dearly loves us as we come to His throne of grace. We want to please Him, not out of fear but from a heart of reciprocal love. When troubles come, we have more confidence because we trust that our Father knows perfectly, loves deeply, and will give us what we need. We may have viewed God as a celestial policeman who was waiting for us to mess up so he could nail us, a harsh judge who loved to shame us, or a distant uncle who really wasn't involved in our lives . . . but no longer.

Some would argue that those who have painful relationships with their fathers can't grasp the love of God as our Father, but I can assure you that's not true. Certainly, men who had loving, strong, supportive dads can more readily make the connection to the God portrayed in the Scriptures. They can compare God to their dads, but people like me can draw a contrast and come to the right conclusions: God is loving, unlike my dad when I was younger; God is patient, unlike him; God is wise, supportive, gentle, and present, unlike my father. I can get to the same right view of the Father, even if I have to take a different route.

Who qualifies to be a child of God? In one sense, none of us, but in another, anyone. Paul explained to the Galatians, "For in Christ Jesus you are all sons of God, through faith. For as many of you as were baptized into Christ have put on Christ. There is neither Jew nor Greek, there is neither slave nor free, there is no male and female, for you are all one in Christ Jesus" (Galatians 3:26-28). If you've come to faith in Jesus, the Father is your Father.

THE CODE OF THE KINGDOM

Every organization has a code of conduct and a code of ethics. Sometimes it's carefully crafted and written for all to see, but sometimes it's assumed. One of the reasons the SEALs are such a cohesive fighting force is that their code is buried deep in each man's soul. These are the statements they live by:

- Loyalty to Country, Team, and Teammate
- Serve with Honor and Integrity On and Off the Battlefield
- Ready to Lead, Ready to Follow, Never Quit
- Take Responsibility for Your Actions and the Actions of Your Teammates
- Excel as Warriors through Discipline and Innovation
- Train for War, Fight to Win, Defeat Our Nation's Enemies
- Earn Your Trident Every Day

A longer statement describes these commitments in more detail. It's a long quote, but you'll see why I believe the full text helps us understand their passion for the task and each other. This is a commitment each man lives by, and if necessary, dies by:

> In times of war or uncertainty there is a special breed of warrior ready to answer our Nation's call. A common man with uncommon desire to succeed.
>
> Forged by adversity, he stands alongside America's finest special operations forces to serve his country, the American people, and protect their way of life.
>
> I am that man.
>
> My Trident is a symbol of honor and heritage. Bestowed upon me by the heroes that have gone before, it embodies the trust of those I have sworn to protect. By wearing the Trident I accept the responsibility of my chosen profession and way of life. It is a privilege that I must earn every day.
>
> My loyalty to Country and Team is beyond reproach. I humbly serve as a guardian to my fellow Americans

always ready to defend those who are unable to defend themselves. I do not advertise the nature of my work, nor seek recognition for my actions. I voluntarily accept the inherent hazards of my profession, placing the welfare and security of others before my own.

I serve with honor on and off the battlefield. The ability to control my emotions and my actions, regardless of circumstance, sets me apart from other men.

Uncompromising integrity is my standard. My character and honor are steadfast. My word is my bond.

We expect to lead and be led. In the absence of orders I will take charge, lead my teammates and accomplish the mission. I lead by example in all situations.

I will never quit. I persevere and thrive on adversity. My Nation expects me to be physically harder and mentally stronger than my enemies. If knocked down, I will get back up, every time. I will draw on every remaining ounce of strength to protect my teammates and to accomplish our mission. I am never out of the fight.

We demand discipline. We expect innovation. The lives of my teammates and the success of our mission depend on me—my technical skill, tactical proficiency, and attention to detail. My training is never complete.

We train for war and fight to win. I stand ready to bring the full spectrum of combat power to bear in order to achieve my mission and the goals established by my country. The execution of my duties will be swift and violent when required yet guided by the very principles that I serve to defend.

Brave men have fought and died building the proud tradition and feared reputation that I am bound to uphold. In the worst of conditions, the legacy of my teammates steadies my resolve and silently guides my every deed. I will not fail.

What is the code for Christians? Some have pointed to the Ten Commandments and the Great Commandment. I wouldn't argue with that, but it's instructive to look at one that comes from the lips of Jesus. The set of characteristics is called The Beatitudes, and it begins Jesus' Sermon on the Mount. Years ago, an English pastor named David Martin Lloyd-Jones preached on this passage and shared an insight:

- The first three, "Blessed are the poor in spirit, for theirs is the kingdom of heaven. Blessed are those who mourn, for they shall be comforted. Blessed are the meek, for they shall inherit the earth" (Matthew 5:3-5), describe our desperate need for Jesus. When we're aware of our sins, our lostness, our hopelessness apart from him, we realize we're utterly bankrupt in spirit and have nothing we can use to impress God. We mourn because we grieve our condition, and we're meek [humble] because self-dependence has brought us to the end of ourselves.

- The next one says, "Blessed are those who hunger and thirst for righteousness, for they shall be satisfied" (v. 6). When we experience the love, forgiveness, acceptance, and power of God through the gospel of Christ, our hunger is satisfied, but we long for more; our thirst is quenched, but we can't get enough of God. We're deeply satisfied, but we're driven to know and love God even more.

■ The next three demonstrate what a grace-drenched, God-satisfied life looks like: "Blessed are the merciful, for they shall receive mercy. Blessed are the pure in heart, for they shall see God. Blessed are the peacemakers, for they shall be called sons of God. Blessed are those who are persecuted for righteousness' sake, for theirs is the kingdom of heaven. Blessed are you when others revile you and persecute you and utter all kinds of evil against you falsely on my account" (vv. 7-11). The connection isn't hard to see: people who have been the recipients of mercy are filled to overflowing with mercy for those who have messed up their lives. Those whose hearts have been cleansed by the blood of Jesus grasp at least a bit of the wonder of God's nature. Those who had been enemies of God but have been made His friends have the wisdom and strength to step into conflict and bring peace. And those who have looked at the unjust punishment Jesus bore for them are willing to pay any price for him.

Jesus' code of the kingdom aren't just platitudes—they propel action, but it's action that reflects the upside-down nature of the kingdom of God. When we live according to this code, we're salt and light. In the ancient world, salt was used for two purposes: to flavor food and as a preservative. When the gospel of grace flows through us, we leave a taste in people's mouths. Some of them find the love of God delicious, but some find it nauseating— their response to us is just like people responded to Jesus. And we're "the light of the world. A city set on a hill cannot be hidden. Nor do people light a lamp and put it under a basket, but on a stand, and it gives light to all in the house. In the same way, let your light shine before others, so that they may see your good works and give glory to your Father who is in heaven" (vv. 13-16). We're spotlights that shine on Jesus, not ourselves.

The question we always need to ask when we're studying the Bible is one we've asked before (and we may ask again): Who is the hero of this story?

The question we always need to ask when we're studying the Bible is one we've asked before (and we may ask again): Who is the hero of this story? We don't have to look far. Who is the one who wasn't just poor in spirit but was crushed in spirit? In the Garden of Gethsemane, Jesus was in anguish "to the point of death" as He looked into the abyss of hell and saw all the punishment He would endure for our sake. Who is the one who mourned? On the cross, Jesus was tortured by His enemies and abandoned by most of His friends. Who is meek? Jesus humbled himself to the point of death, even the humiliating death on a cross. Who hungered and thirsted for righteousness? Jesus often got away to be with the Father, but on the cross, when He was thirsty, they gave Him vinegar. Who is merciful? Mercy is when we don't get what we deserve, and on the cross, Jesus took the pain and separation we deserve. Who is pure in heart? Jesus was sinless, but He hung between two rebels. Who is a peacemaker? Jesus' death took away the barrier between us and God so we could experience His great love. Who was persecuted for righteousness, reviled, mocked, and shamed? We deserved all of that, but Jesus stepped in front and said, "Take me. I'll pay it all." We're not the heroes of the Beatitudes. Someone else surely is.

This is our code. Like the SEALs, it's about a lot more than external conduct—it's grounded in love and loyalty, the twin pillars of a world-changing group of people.

BOOT CAMP

In each of the military services, boot camp is a radical reorientation of identity. Former Marine Morgan DeBusk-Lane looks back on his experience and the impact on everyone in training:

> Regardless of who you are, how smart you are, or what job you have, you are molded, formed, and presented as a uniform character of like resemblance to both the brother to your right and to your left. Through discipline, uniformity was pervasive. This mentality is explained simply as their definition of discipline reads: the instant willingness and obedience to all orders, respect for authority, and self-reliance. You might ask why? . . . simple, because in combat, decisions are made that often counter survival tendencies, defy logic, and are time sensitive—no time to ask why.
>
> If you ask any Marine what they love about being a Marine, they'll likely respond with organizational loyalty and the brotherhood for fellow Marines—social identities—positive ones at that.[16]

When I enlisted, it was a way to escape the pain of my childhood. In only a few weeks, a transformation happened internally and externally. I had a new sense of purpose, a greater sense of pride, a higher degree of confidence in myself . . . and I had a new family of people who were committed to live and die for each other. I'm not sure everyone in boot camp experiences the radical change I did, but mine was very real. Let me explain . . .

When I got off the bus at the Great Lakes Naval Training Center, I was seventeen—it was only the second time I'd ever been away from home. I was a street kid. Even as a little boy in Philadelphia, I ran the streets with my buddies. We were our own neighborhood gang. When our family moved to Delaware when I was in the fifth grade, I made some new friends. We thought of ourselves as "the bowery boys"—tough, proud, and often destructive. In high school, as my family disintegrated, I lived in my own world of alcohol, drugs, cigarettes, and sex. In the first days at Great Lakes, my head was shaved, boots replaced my flip flops, and my shorts and tank tops were put away as I wore the nation's uniform. I'd been playing in a heavy metal rock band, but now that rebellious, self-obsessed lifestyle was over. On the very first day, the recruit division commanders had us stand in front of our bunks. I looked to the left and the right, and I realized, "Man, all of us look just alike! We're clones! This is weird!" But it wasn't weird; it was necessary.

The eight-week curriculum is designed to strip away our old identity and infuse a new one. Physical fitness, weapons training, force protection, and obeying orders without questioning are just some elements of the process. As it progresses, recruits learn to depend on their instructors and each other. By the end, many people experience a transformation similar to mine, and they're much better off for it.

Early in the Gospels, John the Baptist was the star of the show. He looked and acted like an Old Testament prophet had walked onto the scene, and thousands came to hear him preach and be baptized. Then Jesus came, and everything changed for John. Some of his followers wondered why he was suddenly taking a supporting role. He answered, "A person cannot receive even one thing unless it is given him from heaven. You yourselves bear me witness, that I said, 'I am not the Christ, but I have been sent before him.' The one who has the bride is the bridegroom. The friend of the bridegroom, who stands and hears him, rejoices greatly at the bridegroom's voice. Therefore this joy of mine is now complete. He must increase, but I must decrease" (John 3:27-30). John realized that his identity was secondary, and his role was to point people to Jesus. That's the transformation for us, too. Our old identity is now secondary. We used to want to play the starring role, but now that Jesus has shown up in our lives, we don't stay in the spotlight. The question we have to ask—and ask often—is: "Who is worthy of the spotlight, me or Jesus?" We may think the answer is obvious, but whose agenda is more important? Whose fame is our aim? Whose reputation is first in our hearts and on our lips?

I believe suffering is a boot camp for all of us. It's where our selfish assumptions are stripped away and replaced with deeper truth about God and ourselves. Boot camp is hard, but it's productive . . . unless someone bails out because it's more than they expected. In the same way, suffering produces more resilience, deeper faith, and greater insights—as long as we don't bail out too soon.

In the military, soldiers, sailors, and airmen wear insignia. Today, tattoos are very popular in much of our society, but did you know that God has tats? Isaiah tells us about it. God's people had messed up royally. They had worshipped idols, formed alliances with other countries instead of trusting God to protect them, and had a series of incompetent and evil kings. God sent the Babylonians to discipline them, and they did a pretty good job! They destroyed Jerusalem and the temple, killed a lot of people, and hauled many others back to Babylon. God's people complained, "The Lord has forsaken me; my Lord has forgotten me" (Isaiah 49:14).

In reply, God assured them that they were still on His mind . . . and on His hands:

> "Can a woman forget her nursing child,
>> that she should have no compassion on the son of her
>> womb?
> Even these may forget,
>> yet I will not forget you.
> Behold, I have engraved you on the palms of my hands;
>> your walls are continually before me.
> Your builders make haste;
>> your destroyers and those who laid you waste go out
>> from you.
> Lift up your eyes around and see;
>> they all gather, they come to you.
> As I live, declares the Lord,
>> you shall put them all on as an ornament;
>> you shall bind them on as a bride does." (vv.15-18)

Your name and mine are tattooed on God's palms! Even in our darkest moments, even when our sins have caused those dark times, He hasn't forgotten us. He wants us to look up, look to Him, and realize God will have the victory—maybe not in the time we want or the way we expect, but we'll wear God's answers with joy like a bride wears her jewelry . . . and like a soldier, sailor, or airman wears a coveted medal.

Your name and mine are tattooed on God's palms!

CLAIM THE NAME

Every minute of every day, we're children in God's family who have the choice to *claim the name* or *shame the name*. He has gone to the greatest extent to rescue us, redeem us, restore us, and make us His own. God didn't dab a little grace on us, so we don't have to do anything to get more of it. In the opening of Paul's letter to the Ephesians, he says that God has "lavished" the riches of His grace on us.

We can come up with all kinds of excuses to drift instead of holding tight to God. Years ago, Dave gave me a framed quote that has meant a lot to me. It says:

> *"Never be defined by your past. It was a lesson, not a life sentence."*

I look at this profound statement every day. I used to define myself by my crazy, loveless childhood. Dave's words remind me that my past doesn't have to smother me and ruin my life. In fact, I can learn some of life's most important lessons by grieving the losses, experiencing God's healing, and praising Him that His love is personal, infinite, and strong.

We belong to the King, so we're royalty. We didn't earn it, and we don't deserve it—it's a free gift. Princes Charles, William, and Harry realize they didn't earn their place in the pecking order to be King of England. They were born into it. In the same way, we're born into our royal position in God's family. Peter must have learned his lessons well after Jesus restored him on the shore that morning. In his first letter, he assures us, "Blessed be the God and Father of our Lord Jesus Christ! According to his great mercy, he has caused us to be born again to a living hope through the resurrection of Jesus Christ from the dead, to an inheritance that is imperishable, undefiled, and unfading, kept in heaven for you, who by God's power are being guarded through faith for a salvation ready to be revealed in the last time" (1 Peter 1:3-5). It looks like he got the point Jesus was making when He asked Peter three times, "Do you love me?"

What is our inheritance? It's far greater than we can ever imagine. We may worry about our finances and possessions now, whether we can pay the bills, and how we'll retire, but God has promised that someday, in the new heavens and new earth, all things will be made right. In a sermon delivered during World War II, C. S. Lewis explained that when the earth is renewed and perfect, five things will happen to us: We'll be with Christ face to face, we'll be transformed to be like Him in His resurrection body, we'll enjoy feasts with the family of God, we'll be welcomed into God's heart, and we'll be given important jobs in the kingdom.[17]

The idea of royalty certainly won't be odd when that future becomes a reality, and if we let it sink in, it doesn't have to be odd now. Don't forget the name—His and yours. Jesus is the Creator, Savior, King, Morning Star, Lion of Judah, Lamb of God, and Servant of all. You and I are royal children, priests who represent God to people and people to God, chosen, adopted, forgiven, and sealed by the Holy Spirit until the day of redemption.

Believe it. It's true.

When Jesus interacted with people, they always had an extreme response: they either adored Him, hated Him, or feared Him. No one shrugged and said, "Hey, He's cool, but He's no big deal." One of the biggest indictments on believers in our culture is that many of us believe Jesus is nice, and it's good to go to church and pray . . . at least occasionally, but we're not shocked and thrilled that the Creator humbled himself to become human and hang on the cross in our place. New Testament scholar N. T. Wright calls us out:

> How can you live with the terrifying thought that the hurricane has become human, that fire has become flesh, that life itself became life and walked in our midst? Christianity either means that, or it means nothing. It is either the most devastating disclosure of the deepest reality of the world, or it is a sham, a nonsense, a bit of deceitful play-acting. Most of us, unable to cope with saying either of those things, condemn ourselves to live in the shallow world in between. We may not be content there, but we don't know how to escape.[18]

What's your view of Jesus? If you're living in the shallows, do you want to escape?

THINK ABOUT IT:

1. How are the SEAL Code and the Code of the Kingdom (the Beatitudes) similar? How are they different?

2. Read the paragraphs about Lloyd-Jones' insights into the three parts of the Beatitudes. What's the difference in our response between seeing the Beatitudes as a list of demands and seeing Jesus as the hero?

3. How is discipleship, especially with a group of dedicated men, similar to and different from boot camp?

4. Do you think you would benefit from something like a spiritual boot camp? Explain your answer.

5. How might you apply John the Baptist's statement to your life: "Jesus must increase and I must decrease"? Be specific.

6. What are some ways you can apply the message Dave gave me: "Never be defined by your past. It was a lesson, not a life sentence."

CHAPTER 6

The Grace

For the grace of God has appeared, bringing salvation for all people, training us to renounce ungodliness and worldly passions, and to live self-controlled, upright, and godly lives in the present age, waiting for our blessed hope, the appearing of the glory of our great God and Savior Jesus Christ, who gave himself for us to redeem us from all lawlessness and to purify for himself a people for his own possession who are zealous for good works.

—Titus 2:11-14

> Your worst days are never so bad that you are beyond the reach of God's grace. And your best days are never so good that you are beyond the need of God's grace.
>
> —Jerry Bridges

Grace is the purest, simplest concept in theology—it's often explained using the acronym: God's Riches At Christ's Expense. It's a free gift, and who doesn't want something wonderful for free? Actually, it turns out quite a lot of us don't want it. Like the old Smith-Barney commercial, we'd rather "*earn* it." But of course, any attempts to earn God's favor is a rejection of His grace.

I know. I've been there. For many years, everything in me insisted on earning everything meaningful: awards, promotions, opportunities, money, and even friendships. I saw every moment as a test to see if I could excel, and my standards were over the top. There's certainly nothing wrong with the desire to do a good job, but measuring everything by our performance (even our relationship with God) misses the wonder of God's unconditional love, forgiveness, and acceptance, which is the true source of our motivation to obey Him.

In my own life and in the lives of many men who have told me their stories, God seems to use particularly difficult moments to strip away our self-sufficiency so we'll be open to more of His grace. When Sung looked past my flaws and told me she saw "the finished work of God" in my life, it was one of those breakthroughs. The day in Tampa that God led me to run to Grace Street and confront my depravity was another time when He used the dark velvet backdrop of my sin to show the brilliant diamond of His unconditional love.

When I trusted in Christ for my salvation, I knew I was forgiven, but that was just the beginning of God's unveiling His grace to me. Ironically, those who have walked with God intimately and consistently are even more aware of how much they need to learn. In a wonderful prayer in the middle of Paul's letter to the Ephesians, he asks the Father for the Holy Spirit's strength so we can experience His love . . . a love that is far greater than we can imagine. Here's his prayer:

> For this reason I bow my knees before the Father, from whom every family in heaven and on earth is named, that according to the riches of his glory he may grant you to be strengthened with power through his Spirit in your inner being, so that Christ may dwell in your hearts through faith—that you, being rooted and grounded in love, may

have strength to comprehend with all the saints what is the breadth and length and height and depth, and to know the love of Christ that surpasses knowledge, that you may be filled with all the fullness of God. (Ephesians 3:14-19)

Grace isn't some mushy, sentimental thing. It's combined with the immeasurable power of Almighty God to transform us from the inside out . . . and it's beyond comprehension, as we long to experience as much of it as we possibly can. In other words, grace is a bottomless well. And it changes hearts. I remember when one of my sons disobeyed me. He apologized, but he expected me to lean on him. Instead, I said, "I forgive you. Let's go get some ice cream."

In other words, grace is a bottomless well. And it changes hearts.

He looked stunned and asked, "Aren't you going to ground me? Aren't you taking away my video games for a while?"

I answered, "Why would I do that? You came to me, you admitted what you did, and I forgive you. Done. Over. What flavor do you want?"

He shook his head and insisted, "But Dad, I don't deserve ice cream."

"That's right, son," I explained. "That's what God's grace looks like."

It was a small but significant way to teach him about grace. Actually, we sometimes use mercy and grace interchangeably, but they're different. Mercy means that we don't get what we deserve (punishment for our sins); grace means that and more—that we get what we don't deserve (adoption, Christ's righteous standing before the Father, love, and acceptance). Thankfully, God gives us both in abundance. When I didn't ground my son, that was mercy. When we went out for ice cream, that was grace.

TWO SONS

When we read the familiar parable of the Prodigal Son in Luke's Gospel, we often focus on only one relationship: the wayward young man and his gracious dad. However, I think we should call it "the parable of the two lost sons." You know the story Jesus told: A man had two sons. The younger son couldn't stand staying home any longer. He asked his father for his share of the inheritance so he could leave town and live his own life with no restrictions. In that day, the oldest son in the family received a double portion of the inheritance, so the younger son in the parable would have received one-third of the estate after his father died. But stop right there. Wealth wasn't held in stocks or bank accounts. This means that the father would have to liquidate land and livestock to grant the son's request, a humbling thing for any landowner to do. And even worse, asking for his share of the estate indicates that the younger son wished his father was dead! It's hard to imagine a more hurtful demand.

The young man took off to a place far from home where he "squandered his property in reckless living" (Luke 15:13). We don't have to use our imaginations very much to figure what that lifestyle may have looked like for him! But later, when a famine ravaged the land, the young man had nothing to fall back on. He was both physically and spiritually bankrupt. This Jewish kid worked the only job available: feeding pigs and salivating as he looked at the slop the pigs were eating. How low can you go?

This guy was at the bottom, but "he came to himself" and realized his father's hired servants had plenty to eat. He crafted a plan to go home and ask for a job. He didn't have any hope that he would be restored as a son—he had blown that to bits! On his way back, he most likely rehearsed his confession and his plea.

Meanwhile, his dad had obviously been looking down the road every day, hoping to see his son coming home. When he finally saw him, this patriarchal figure of dignity hiked up his robes and ran like the wind toward his son. Can you imagine what the boy must have thought? *He's coming to kill me!* But the father threw his arms around him and kissed him. The young man started into his speech, but his father interrupted him, telling the servants, "Bring quickly the best robe, and put it on him, and put a ring on his hand, and shoes on his feet. And bring the fattened calf and kill it, and let us eat and celebrate. For this my son was dead, and is alive again; he was lost, and is found." And then, the celebration began (vv. 22-24).

Robes were very expensive and were often part of an inheritance—the dad replaced his son's tattered, pig-smelling rags with the finest robe in the house. A signet ring was used to make a mark on contracts, so the young man was restored to a full member of the family. He had probably come barefooted, and his father gave him comfortable shoes to wear. And then, the best part—his father told the servants to prepare for the greatest feast the town had ever had! There was no condemnation, no demand for payback, no withdrawal of love . . . just the opposite.

But that's not the end of the story. The older son was working in the fields. When he heard the commotion, he asked one of the servants what was going on. When he heard that his brother, the one who had shamed him and his father, had come home—and was warmly welcomed back—he was furious! He refused to go to the party. His father came out to invite him to come, but this son barked at him, "Look, these many years I have served you, and I never disobeyed your command, yet you never gave me a young goat, that I might celebrate with my friends. But when this son of yours came, who has devoured your property with prostitutes, you killed the fattened calf for him!" (vv. 29-30)

In a gracious and tender moment, his father pleaded with him, "Son, you are always with me, and all that is mine is yours. It was fitting to celebrate and be glad, for this your brother was dead, and is alive; he was lost, and is found" (vv. 31-32).

Do you sense the older son's outrage at the grace his father showed his brother? He wouldn't even call him "my brother," but called him "your son." His defense was that he had served, obeyed, and labored for his father, and as the only remaining son, he expected to have the entire inheritance. His brother deserved nothing; he deserved it all . . . or so he thought. He had tried to earn his place by being good and working hard, but he had completely missed his father's heart. The younger son had tried to find life and fulfillment by disobeying his father, but the older son tried to make life work by trusting in his obedience and hard work. In the end, only one of them enjoyed the overflowing love of their father . . . and it wasn't the self-righteous, hard-working, rigidly obedient son!

In virtually every group and every family, we find both kinds of people. Some of us have fled "to a far country" of self-indulgence and rebellion, but we've come to our senses, turned back to God, and experienced the joy of His welcome. Others have gone to church regularly, served faithfully, and given sacrificially, but they've missed the Father's heart. They've tried to earn His love by being decent, trying hard, and being good, but it has left them empty, and worse, full of self-pity and resentment.

In virtually every group and every family, we find both kinds of people.

I believe grace is so hard to truly grasp that many Christians are somewhere on an "older brother" continuum. Legalism is the confidence that following rigid rules earns points with God—like the Pharisees in the Gospels. Moralism is like it, but different. It's the confidence that being a "good enough" person is what God is looking for, but how good is really enough? No one can be sure. All of us are tempted to lean into moralism, to assume our good performance makes us acceptable to God . . . or at least a little more acceptable, but that's getting the order wrong. The pattern of moralism is "we obey so we're accepted," but the order of grace is "we're accepted so we obey." The wrong order focuses on us and our performance, and it inevitably produces pride and fear; the right order focuses on God and produces gratitude and joy. It makes a world of difference!

People perceive the Christian life in three ways: the grind, the platform, or the wonder. The older brother saw his life as a grind.

He worked hard, but there was no joy, no gratitude, no love. He believed his hard work and discipline were enough to earn plenty of points with his dad, but he missed out on the love his father had for him. His whole life revolved around his performance, and it left him empty.

Some people are looking for a platform to show what they can do, or to have power over others. Life isn't a grind for them; it's a stage where they can perform to earn applause. When they get acclaim, they feel great about themselves, but when they don't, they blame others or slink into despair . . . at least until the curtain goes up on the next act.

But others see their lives as nothing short of wonderful. They're amazed that God would love and care enough about them to pursue them, rescue them, and love them. I can imagine the younger brother's relationship with his dad after the parable ends. I envision him being overwhelmed with his father's forgiveness and generosity, and I can see them walking together to share affection they missed while he was away. (And I can hear him tell stories about what it was like feeding pigs!)

Listen, I know grace is counterintuitive. We earn grades in school, we earn a spot on a team, we earn awards, we earn positions, and we earn a salary. Grace isn't like anything else in our world. That's why we slip so easily into moralism, and that's why we need to keep coming back to the wonders of grace.

GRACE IN—GRACE OUT

Jesus often taught the disciples about forgiveness and grace. In their culture, forgiveness was given hesitantly. One time Peter asked, "Lord, how often will my brother sin against me, and I forgive him? As many as seven times?"

Jesus gave an astonishing reply, "I do not say to you seven times, but seventy-seven times" (Matthew 18:21-22). His point wasn't to count: "seventy-six, seventy-seven, done . . . no more forgiveness." Instead, His implication was to "forgive extravagantly as many times as necessary." To illustrate His point, He told a parable about a king and a servant. The servant was in debt to the king the astronomical amount of ten thousand talents. A talent was a measure of gold or silver weighing about seventy pounds. Scholars estimate that this amount equates to trillions of dollars. Jesus' point is that the debt was utterly overwhelming and impossible to repay. This servant wasn't a butler or a gardener. To owe this kind of money meant that he must have had a high position, like Secretary of the Treasury, and he had either mismanaged the king's money or committed fraud.

The king ordered the servant and his family to be sold, which wouldn't come close to wiping out the debt, but was his only recourse. The servant pleaded for patience, and he promised to pay it all back. Instead, the king forgave him and canceled the debt. That's a wonderful story, but Jesus wanted to make a bigger point.

The servant walked away a free man, but when he saw another servant who owed him a few thousand dollars, he grabbed him and demanded, "Pay back what you owe." The second servant pleaded with him in the same way he had pleaded with the king, but the one who had received an enormous amount of grace wouldn't give even a little grace to someone else. He had the man thrown in debtors' prison until he paid his debt.

Other servants knew of the king's grace to the first servant, and they saw his cruelty to the second servant. They told the king what happened, and the king told the first servant, "You wicked servant! I forgave you all that debt because you pleaded with me. And should not you have had mercy on your fellow servant, as I had mercy on you?" (vv. 32-33)

Jesus concluded the lesson: "And in anger his master delivered him to the jailers, until he should pay all his debt. So also my heavenly Father will do to every one of you, if you do not forgive your brother from your heart" (vv. 34-35).

Sin creates a debt, and we owed God a debt that couldn't possibly be repaid, but He has graciously forgiven us. The entire debt is canceled and we've been set free, but how do we treat people who have done something to hurt us?

Do you get it? You and I are the first servant. Sin creates a debt, and we owed God a debt that couldn't possibly be repaid, but He has graciously forgiven us. The entire debt is canceled and we've been set free, but how do we treat people who have done something to hurt us? Do we figuratively grab them and demand they pay their debt, or do we remember how much we're forgiven and pay it forward? I'm not in any way minimizing the debt some people may owe us. Some have been physically, emotionally, or sexually abused; some have been abandoned and unloved; and others have been betrayed by those they trusted. These are deep wounds and big debts, but when we consider the debt Jesus paid for us, we'll have more resources to forgive the debts of those who have hurt us. It may take time to grieve as we forgive, but the more we drink in God's grace, the more it flows out of us.

GRACELESS POLITICS

I'm glad you've read a lot of the book up to this point because I'm afraid I'm going to lose a few people now. One of the things that has concerned me in the past few years is that a lot of believers identify much more strongly with a political party and particular politicians than Jesus and the kingdom of God. To me, it's irrefutable—I've seen and heard countless Christians speak more passionately (and often angrily) about politics than about the love and grace of God.

Don't get me wrong. I'm not saying that abortion, immigration, energy policy, taxes, guns, and all the other issues aren't important. They're important, but not as essential as Jesus and His kingdom of kindness, justice, and righteousness. From a political standpoint I tend to lean conservative, but I'm a Christian first. You may be a progressive, but if you're a believer, you're a Christian first. Some of the most hateful language I've heard has come from the lips of Christians. Salt and light? No, it's garbage and darkness.

People are watching. In our culture, our loud and angry political discourse has, for many, clouded our witness for Christ. And the intense polarization makes it even worse. To even acknowledge that the other side may have a small, reasonable point is to invite wrath from "true believers." Peter Wehner is a conservative Christian columnist who observes:

> The enthusiastic, uncritical embrace of President Trump by white evangelicals is among the most mind-blowing developments of the Trump era. How can a group that for decades—and especially during the Bill Clinton presidency—insisted that character counts and that personal integrity is an essential component of presidential leadership not only turn a blind eye to the ethical and moral transgressions of Donald Trump, but also constantly defend him? Why are those who have been on the vanguard of "family values" so eager to give a man with a sordid personal and sexual history a mulligan?

Wehner describes the price we pay for putting politics ahead of our devotion to God:

> There's a very high cost to our politics for celebrating the Trump style, but what is most personally painful to me as a person of the Christian faith is the cost to the Christian witness. Nonchalantly jettisoning the ethic of Jesus in favor of a political leader who embraces the ethic of Thrasymachus and Nietzsche—might makes right, the strong should rule over the weak, justice has no intrinsic worth, moral values are socially constructed and subjective—is troubling enough.[19]

Studies by Pew Research and FiveThirtyEight show that younger Americans are leaving the church in droves. They believe older Christians don't care about racial injustice, income inequality, climate change, and gun violence, among other topics important to them. They see many Christian leaders defending behavior they consider indefensible, and they're repulsed.[20]

Yes, we can argue, "But what about the liberals?" Progressives certainly promote policies that aren't in line with Scripture. There's no doubt about that, but instead of loud condemnations, we should offer better alternatives. We need to learn to disagree with someone without hating them. Jesus teaches us to love our enemies, befriend the strangers, and care for the marginalized. Can't we figure out how to stand for biblical values without resorting to behavior that is far, far from the heart of Jesus? I think we can. I think we must.

The real problem isn't that *other people* identify us with ultra-right-wing positions and conspiracy theories; the real problem is that *many of us* actually (and happily) embrace those positions and theories.

If people hate me because they see that I'm communicating the love of Jesus in word and actions, I'm completely fine with that. But if they hate me because I've taken a rabid political stance cloaked in Christian terms, I've misrepresented Jesus to them. In a message on the resurrection, pastor Tim Keller remarked that many people in our churches haven't really embraced Jesus . . . they've embraced their agenda for Jesus.[21] What is that agenda? In Mark's Gospel, each time Jesus predicted His death and resurrection, the disciples either disputed Him (Peter), argued about who would be the greatest in His coming kingdom (all of them), or asked for the highest places of authority and privilege (James and John). Their agenda completely missed the point! Jesus called them (and us) to deny our selfish agendas, take up our crosses of humility, sacrifice, and love for enemies and outsiders, and follow Him in a cross-shaped attitude and life.

Anger can be righteous or unrighteous. It's good and right when we're angry about injustice but we love the sinners; it's bad and wrong when we're upset about not getting the power and privilege we think we deserve. There can't be a clearer illustration of a cross-shaped life than this: Jesus gave up His power and privilege to love sinners "to the uttermost." That's His call for us, too. Our hearts become hardened by our insistence on our rights, but they're melted and molded into the image of Jesus by our experience of His love, grace, and kindness.

Grace. It's precious, powerful, and rare. No other religion has anything like it. The rest are moral philosophies or legalistic standards. The famous English pastor Charles Spurgeon commented, "Nothing but grace makes a man so humble and, at the same time, so glad." Writer Flannery O'Connor wrote, "All human nature vigorously resists grace because grace changes us and the change is painful."

Are you willing to stop resisting grace and let its power change you from the inside out? That's what God wants for all of us . . . even you and me.

THINK ABOUT IT:

1. Explain how you think God works in people to help them experience His grace. Is it episodic as difficult events strip away our self-sufficiency, or is it more gradual as we read His Word and pray? Which of these has God used in your life?

2. How would you summarize Jesus' point about the older brother in the parable of the two sons?

3. For you, is the Christian life more of a grind, a platform to win applause, or a wonder that God's grace has reached even you? Explain your answer.

4. When and why do you sometimes act like the first servant in Jesus story in Matthew 18? (We all do.) What does that tell you about your grasp of grace?

5. Who do you know who experiences and expresses grace to a great degree? Do you know how that person has come to that understanding? What impact does he or she have on others, including you?

6. Did I lose you in the section on graceless politics? What merit, if any, do you see in my position?

CHAPTER 7

The Resilient

But we have this treasure in jars of clay, to show that the surpassing power belongs to God and not to us. We are afflicted in every way, but not crushed; perplexed, but not driven to despair; persecuted, but not forsaken; struck down, but not destroyed; always carrying in the body the death of Jesus, so that the life of Jesus may also be manifested in our bodies.

—2 Corinthians 4:7-10

Circumstances which we have resented, situations which we have found desperately difficult, have all been the means in the hands of God of driving the nails into the self-life which so easily complains.

—Alan Redpath

My disappointment in having to drop out of SEAL training was tempered a little by the hope that I'd get back there after my tailbone healed and I finished my deployment . . . but only a little. To be honest, it took me a long time to come to grips with the death of my dream. I wasn't going to let my goal vanish because I took a bump on my rear end! I doubled down on staying fit and ready, but it was difficult when I was working eighteen-hour shifts on a destroyer. After I left the Navy, I became just as dedicated and disciplined to get a college degree and excel in business. Being full-on and full-out didn't give me space to reflect on my loss, and that suited me just fine.

Years later, when I was able to step back and look at things from God's perspective, I realized that God's purpose for me is far bigger and better—and different—than my agenda. The goal of Christian life isn't getting God on my schedule and plan; it's aligning my agenda and plan with His. And I saw that even if I'd stayed and completed the training, life may not have worked out the way I hoped. The Officer in Charge in our class was killed in a training accident soon after he completed BUD/S, including Hell Week and the dive phase. During SEAL qualification exercises, students receive training in explosives and demolition. That's when the accident took his life. I heard about guys who dropped out of BUD/S and committed suicide, and I knew of guys who were on SEAL team missions and were killed in action. Others who had retired from service struggled to cope with the trauma they'd experienced on the battlefield, and they had difficulty adjusting to life back home. Their entire identity was wrapped up in being a SEAL. Who were they now? I could have been one of those guys—killed in training, killed in action, or struggling to cope. At least I was alive and of reasonably sound mind. That was something. I concluded that God still had something for me.

Trusting God wasn't easy for me (and isn't for anyone else, for that matter). I'd always advanced by performing well, and I brought that perspective into my walk with Christ. I was determined to be the most faithful group member, most pleasant usher, most outstanding youth pastor, and best preacher anyone ever saw, but all of that was driven by the expectation that it would earn points with people and with God. I believed I was saved by grace, but it ended there. I had no idea how grace could transform my motivations so I could do all those things out of gratitude instead of seeing them as rungs on a ladder of acceptance.

God used seminal events to get my attention, knock the props out from under me, show me how much I need Him every moment of every day, and demonstrate that He is all I need.

By this point in the book, you've obviously picked up on the fact that I only learn the hard way. God used seminal events to get my attention, knock the props out from under me, show me how much I need Him every moment of every day, and demonstrate that He is all I need. One of those events was the leaders' weekend in Tampa when God sent me out for a run to Grace Street. As I thought about those two days in the hotel while I was strung out, I remembered that I had written a letter to Sung and the children. I don't remember the exact contents of the letter since I threw it out immediately after I woke up, but I remember that I explained that if they were reading the letter, it meant that I hadn't woken up from a night of partying and depravity, I was sorry, and I loved them very much. The letter was sad enough, but even more depressing was the fact that I had partied so much that I wasn't able to call them to say goodnight—something that haunts me to this day.

The next morning, my phone rang. It was Sung, and she was frantic. Through my mental haze, I tried to figure out what to say that would make sense without giving anything away. I glanced over at the bedside table. There was the letter. I had lived through the night, so they didn't need to ever read it. Sung asked why I hadn't called or answered her calls. That's when I came up with the story that I'd left my phone in the rental car and had just gotten it back . . . early in the morning when it was exceptionally unlikely that this would be the moment the rental car company would have gotten it to me. It was the best I could come up with at the time.

Then, years later when Sung and I were at the Tampa leadership event and God sent me for the run, I finally—finally—was able to be completely honest with God, myself, Sung, and the others at the event. That day was a turning point. Paradoxically, true resilience has resulted from giving up on my self-improvement project, admitting my brokenness, and embracing God's unconditional love. For too long, I'd tried to control myself . . . and failed miserably. I looked successful on the outside, but I was hurting, desperate, and empty on the inside. That day changed my sense of purpose. I'd been fighting a defensive battle for years, and soldiers on defense seldom win. I'd been consumed with protecting my reputation by lying and deceiving, but now I wanted to please God and honor Him in everything.

"LET'S GO GET 'EM"

Resilience is crafted over years of training—spiritually or militarily—and we can then call on it in the heat of a critical moment. Marc Lee was voted "Class Clown" twice in high school, and he was a star on the soccer field. A committed Christian, he enrolled in a Christian college and played on the soccer team, but he had a dream to become a Navy SEAL. He went to a recruiting office and signed a contract to try out for SEAL training. He was accepted and made it through most of Hell Week. With only hours until it was over, the doctors diagnosed pneumonia and pulmonary edema. He desperately wanted to complete Hell Week, but a man had died of the same condition in a previous class, so he wasn't allowed to continue. He repeated the training sometime later and excelled, ranking second in his class.

As a member of SEAL Team Three, Marc deployed to Iraq in 2006. They were sent to Ramadi, "the worst piece of real estate in Iraq." Allied with other units from the Marines and Army, the SEALs were ordered to set up a Combat Output in the heart of the insurgency-controlled part of the city. The first encounter with heavily armed terrorists was followed by an American counter-attack, resulting in seventeen enemy KIA and dozens wounded. The CO was successfully established.

On the night of August 2, 2006, Marc and his unit engaged in a ferocious firefight, perhaps the most intense in the Battle of Ramadi. While providing covering fire from a housetop with his machine gun, Marc's friend Ryan was shot in the face. His condition was critical. Other members of the team provided immediate medical support while Marc stepped into Ryan's position to lay down covering fire. With this suppression, the other team members got Ryan off the roof and saved his life.

The fight died down and the team went back to its base. A short time later, the Chief walked in and announced a recon team had identified about thirty insurgents that had been on the other side of the firefight. He asked if the team members were willing to go back out. They had just endured a two-hour firefight in 115-degree heat carrying weapons, ammo, and other equipment up to 150 pounds, and their buddy had been severely wounded. Marc told the Chief, "Roger that. Let's go get 'em." They went house to house clearing the area. At the last house, they cleared the first floor, and Marc started up the stairs. He took fire through a window and was instantly killed.

Marc was awarded the Silver Star and Purple Heart for his actions on that night. He also received a Bronze Star for his heroism two weeks earlier when he exposed himself to direct fire to protect his team. His unit became the most decorated of any special ops unit since Vietnam. An article about Marc in a publication by America's Mighty Warriors says: "Marc will always be remembered for his humor, playful antics, determination, perseverance, courage, selfless attitude, and his faith. His headstone reads: 'Loved deeply, deeply loved.'"[22]

Marc Lee is a model of courageous, love-motivated resilience.

READY FOR ANYTHING

I'm afraid a lot of Christians are soft. They read the promises of Scripture, and they expect God to give them a life of complete peace and prosperity. They haven't read enough of the Bible! Yes, God gives us magnificent promises, but many of them are designed to strengthen us when we go through times of suffering and opposition. We're in a very real battle. In some eras of the church, believers were tortured and killed. Today, our battle is to use the resources God has put in our hands to advance the kingdom . . . instead of spending it all on ourselves. In some ways, it's a harder fight because there are fewer true antagonists—we're primarily fighting against our own passivity and selfishness. (I've talked to a number of people who believe Christians in America are being persecuted. I recommend that they do a little more research into the history of the early church and different periods when believers were thrown to lions, had molten lead poured into holes in their skulls, were burned alive, and experienced horrific torture in many other ways. Today, we're facing some opposition for our faith, but nothing like what those people suffered for their willingness to stand up for Jesus.)

> Yes, God gives us magnificent promises, but many of them are designed to strengthen us when we go through times of suffering and opposition.

When SEALs train, they're preparing for any eventuality in battle. They spend far more time getting ready for fights than actually engaging in them, but none of that effort is wasted. Training with their teams gives them confidence in themselves and each other. When our team trained to board ships to look for WMD, our CO presented us with a wide range of contingencies so we'd be ready for anything. If we were surprised, we weren't sufficiently trained.

As a Rescue Swimmer, I had to be ready to pick up pilots of downed helicopters in every conceivable situation. The training wasn't just about rescue techniques; it was about developing the endurance to do the job when you're exhausted but your buddy is in trouble and needs you, and it was about learning to think clearly when you haven't slept for three days. It's the same for fire-fighters, police, plumbers, electricians, accountants, IT specialists . . . and Christians. If we're not adequately trained mentally, phys-ically, and technically, we won't be prepared to react with wisdom and speed in difficult situations. In the military, we develop the attitude that we never quit on the mission or our teammates, but in our Christian walks, we often bail out as soon as we face the slightest inconvenience. We can do better. We have to do better.

Training isn't always pleasant, but it's necessary. Paul tells us to "put on the full armor of God" in Ephesians 6. Peter warns us that we're not fighting a conventional war. It's an insurgency led by a deceptive enemy: "Be sober-minded; be watchful. Your adversary the devil prowls around like a roaring lion, seeking someone to devour. Resist him, firm in your faith, knowing that the same kinds of suffering are being experienced by your broth-erhood throughout the world." But he assures us, "And after you have suffered a little while, the God of all grace, who has called you to his eternal glory in Christ, will himself restore, confirm, strengthen, and establish you" (1 Peter 5:8-10). Paul tells his protégé Timothy, who may have needed the strong encourage-ment from his mentor, "Fight the good fight of the faith. Take hold of the eternal life to which you were called and about which you made the good confession in the presence of many witnesses" (1 Timothy 6:12). The Greek word for *fight* is the same word for *agony*. What is the agony in our fight of faith? It's a lot of things: going against our strong inclinations toward revenge when peo-ple have hurt us, being patient with family members when we're frustrated with them, getting up early to go to a Bible study, listening instead of insisting on being heard, serving people who aren't very grateful, having integrity at work when shading the facts are the norm among our peers, speaking the truth in love instead of cowering in silence or demanding compliance, and on and on. These are hard choices that go against our natural bent. It's a fight to value Jesus above success, pleasure, and approval, and it's our fight all day every day.

In his last letter, Paul uses three professions as metaphors of resilience: a soldier, an athlete, and a farmer. He makes particular points with each one. A soldier is single-minded. "Share in suffering as a good soldier of Christ Jesus. No soldier gets entangled in civilian pursuits, since his aim is to please the one who enlisted him" (2 Timothy 2:3-4). Who is our CO? A boss, a spouse, children, our own desires . . . or God? An athlete is a student of the regulations of competition and follows them if he expects to win. "An athlete is not crowned unless he competes according to the rules" (v. 5). And a farmer labors with the expectation that his work won't be in vain. "It is the hard-working farmer who ought to have the first share of the crops" (v. 6). Paul then says, in effect, "Timothy, your walk of faith has parallels to each of these three professions. Pay attention and learn what they mean for you."

In his previous letter to Timothy, Paul had described the necessity of discipline and training. After instructing Timothy to address the problems of legalism and moralism, Paul told him, "If you put these things before the brothers, you will be a good servant of Christ Jesus, being trained in the words of the faith and of the good doctrine that you have followed. Have nothing to do with irreverent, silly myths. Rather train yourself for godliness;

for while bodily training is of some value, godliness is of value in every way, as it holds promise for the present life and also for the life to come. The saying is trustworthy and deserving of full acceptance. For to this end we toil and strive, because we have our hope set on the living God, who is the Savior of all people, especially of those who believe" (1 Timothy 4:6-10).

People sometimes comment on my physical conditioning and ask if I exercise "all the time." I tell them "no." I certainly exercise and eat healthy foods, but my spiritual training is far more important. Some might look at this passage and expect to be excused: "This was written for a pastor, and I'm not one, so it doesn't apply to me." But it does. In the early church, the leaders were elders, and elders were selected because they were already demonstrating what Paul is talking about. So, training in godliness is for all of us who are disciples of Jesus and royal children of God, whether we're chosen to be elders or not.

I've found that my physical and spiritual training complement each other. I've grown to love the sport of Jiu Jitsu. It has revealed nagging remnants of ego and taught me new depths of humility. My good friend Larry Glines, a neighbor in St. Augustine, introduced me to it. When he invited me to come to his new Jiu Jitsu academy, I wanted to tell him I'd been involved in martial arts since I was a kid, and I'd be happy to come and show him how it's done. (More than a little cocky.) I was his first student. He showed me a few basic moves, which felt pretty familiar to what I'd done for years. I was confident I was not just the first but the most talented student he'd ever have. Then he asked Larry, Jr. to join us. If you asked someone to find a picture of the classic Millennial kid, he was it. He had a "man bun" in his hair, he was a student at the University of Florida, and he weighed about forty pounds less than me. I thought about all the men I'd served with, the physical specimens in SEAL and Rescue Swimmer training, and I immediately concluded, "I'm going to crush this kid!"

Larry set up each bout, or "roll," for five minutes, and then his son and I stepped onto the mat. We gave each other a fist bump, and we were off. We each made a few moves, and then, before the first minute was up, he had me in a compromising position, and I had to tap to give in. You have to understand that I was trained to never quit, so I kept going so long that I was seeing stars and was about to pass out. We got up, took a couple of minutes for me to regroup, and went at it again. In the next four minutes, I did a lot better—I only tapped out once every two minutes instead of once a minute! By the end, I felt totally humiliated. I was also out of breath and utterly exhausted . . . after being taken down by a kid who hadn't gone through any training like I'd experienced. When he was in diapers, I'd been in the military for years, where I learned some sophisticated self-defense tactics. I'd participated in Spartan races, and I'd practiced boxing and Kuk Sool Won for a few years, but I was no match for the skinny kid with the man bun.

That day (and others like it) showed me how judgmental I've been. Just by looking at someone, I sized them up physically, mentally, and psychologically. I'd done that with Larry, Jr., and I was dead wrong. I'd been just as wrong about a lot of other people. I had considered myself to be superior, but I didn't know the whole story about them, and actually, I didn't have the story right about myself either. I wasn't as hot as I thought . . . a revelation that Sung and others had probably prayed about for years!

I wouldn't have seen my glaring pride and judgmental attitude if I hadn't been tested on the mat with Larry, Jr. But testing doesn't end there. God tests me all the time to push me to my limits to reveal what's already there. In times of stress, I don't *become* selfish, angry, and demanding—those traits just come to the surface during the difficult moments. I'm no longer as surprised when the warning light flashes on the dashboard of my soul. In Jiu Jitsu, I've competed at some pretty high levels, and every match, especially the ones I lose, teach me elements of humility I hadn't learned before. Pride prevents learning. Sometimes when Sung and I are cruising along in our marriage and we assume we finally have it down, we have an argument over something that's exceedingly stupid. I want to shout, "Where did *that* come from?" The answer is simple: it comes from our still-somewhat-deceived, still-in-training, not-quite-resilient hearts.

When we think we're beyond correction, we're in deep trouble. I know people who have earned black belts in Jiu Jitsu, and they say they still have so much to learn. Similarly, I know some wonderful people who are giants in the faith who have an accurate self-perception. They aren't at all shocked when their responses to situations and people aren't Christlike. They're humble enough to admit it, ask for forgiveness, and learn the lessons God wants to teach them.

A sensitive, humble heart makes us good at a particular skill that isn't valued as much as it should be: repentance. We're reluctant to repent for two main reasons: we're either arrogant and hard-hearted, assuming we don't need to repent . . . or we're fragile and ashamed by what we've done, and we don't believe God's forgiveness can reach as far as we've fallen. If we believe repentance only exposes our flaws and leaves us vulnerable and guilty, we'll avoid it like the plague. Actually, Paul describes two kinds of repentance. He had written a letter to the Corinthians to point out a major sin and call them to confess and repent. That letter is lost, but we know how they responded because we have his reply to them after he received their response. It's the letter of 2 Corinthians. He wrote:

> For even if I made you grieve with my letter, I do not regret it—though I did regret it, for I see that that letter grieved you, though only for a while. As it is, I rejoice, not because you were grieved, but because you were grieved into repenting. For you felt a godly grief, so that you suffered no loss through us. For godly grief produces a repentance that leads to salvation without regret, whereas worldly grief produces death. (2 Corinthians 7:8-10)

"Worldly grief" is the soul-crushing shame that feeds self-hatred. People who respond this way have a big view of their sin but a very small view of God's love and forgiveness. They think they have to earn forgiveness by feeling bad enough long enough, calling themselves horrible names, and withdrawing from God until they think they've been good enough (which may or may not ever happen).

"Godly grief" is very different. It has an accurate view of sin and an expansive view of God's love and forgiveness. People with this perspective don't avoid repentance. They run toward it because it reaffirms their connection to God and restores their experience of His kindness.

Worldly grief says, "I've really messed up. I can't let Dad know."

Godly grief says, "I've really messed up. I need to call my Dad."

Repentance should be practiced often, even many times a day. It's a way of making mid-course corrections. When a pilot is flying from New York to Los Angeles, he doesn't wait until he's so far off course that he's in Montana before he corrects his heading. He makes thousands of little corrections each time the plane drifts even slightly away from the flight plan. I experienced a perfect example of this when I became an Enlisted Warfare Surface Specialist and wore the insignia on my chest. In a year (more or less) of training and qualifications, the people who earn it become skilled at virtually every aspect of running a destroyer. If, for any reason, the ranking officer is killed or incapacitated, this specialist knows the capabilities and systems of the ship. One of the competencies is, of course, steering the 529-foot ship. When I was in training to become this specialist, I was on the bridge with the quartermaster as the captain watched me. To stay on course, I had to make countless corrections. If the ship stayed on the wrong heading of only one degree, over time we could find ourselves off the coast of the wrong country! The ship has a computer tracking system that shows the actual path of the vessel over a period of time. When I'd finished and they showed me the readout of my time at the helm, I was shocked. It looked like a three-year old had marked it with a pen—the line was all over the place! It wasn't that I'd been distracted or negligent. I'd been laser focused on the path, but I'd gone off course again and again. My corrections sometimes weren't quite enough and other times a bit too much, but I was able to keep us at least generally headed in the right direction.

Repentance is necessary, we need to practice it continually, and it will keep us on track with God and His purposes, but we won't do it perfectly. Sometimes we'll under-correct, and some-times we'll over-correct, but we'll generally stay on God's head-ing. And the people around us are watching. One of the most important practices we can model for our families, coworkers, and friends is the willingness to say those three little words, "I was wrong," coupled with three more, "Please forgive me." For centuries, church services regularly included confession, repen-tance, and assurance of forgiveness. I hope more pastors and other church leaders will find ways to add this emphasis back into their liturgy.

Repentance is necessary, we need to practice it continually, and it will keep us on track with God and His purposes, but we won't do it perfectly. Sometimes we'll under-correct, and sometimes we'll over-correct, but we'll generally stay on God's heading.

BAND OF BROTHERS

When I was a boy, I ran with a bunch that prided itself on being tough. If one of us got in a fight, we all joined in. We looked out for each other. For instance, the father of one of our group was an alcoholic, and when he got violent, his son came to stay at our house or the home of one of the other boys.

Some time ago I took my daughter Tehya to Africa on her first mission trip, and we went on a safari. The guide showed us all kinds of animals, including many kinds of gazelles and lions. He explained that the lions were always looking for a gazelle that was apart from the herd. That made them easy targets. It's the same for us. When we're isolated, we're easy targets for the roaring lion who is "seeking someone to devour."

When I was struggling with alcohol, drugs, and my obsession with business success, I remained isolated by choice. I didn't want anyone to see behind the curtain! I generated a lot of stress, and my coping strategy was to drink and use even more. It was a self-defeating loop. From the day when I was eight years old and my mom gave me a pill when I was upset, I'd used substances to cope with fear, hurt, anger, and anxiety.

In the military, things changed. Training exercises and real actions created a lot of stress, but I learned to rely on the people on my team. We had different responsibilities, but we coordinated our efforts and trusted each other. When I left the service, I started attending a men's Bible study at the church. They were wonderful guys, but I didn't share life-or-death situational training with them. It was easy to go only so deep, but no further. I was afraid to reveal too much of myself too soon, so I missed the bonds I could have formed with them. I thought, *I'll figure it out. And besides, my problems aren't so bad after all.* I read self-help books on discipline and self-improvement, but I didn't realize that genuine, lasting change happens in trusting, vulnerable, honest relationships, not in the pages of a book.

When Jesus chose the Twelve, it seems like He was select-
ing members of a special ops team. They were from very different
backgrounds with very different skills, but He assigned the team
the greatest task ever given—to reach every person on the planet
with the gospel and build God's kingdom on earth. They argued
about who would be the greatest, and they missed His heart
for the marginalized, but He stuck with them, and collectively
(except for one) they turned the world upside down. When Jesus
sent them out, He sent them in pairs so they wouldn't be isolated
and vulnerable to the enemy's attacks and the discouragement of
opposition. They needed each other.

Paul always took someone with him—Barnabas, John Mark,
Silas, Luke, Timothy, and others—so they could share the bur-
dens and the joys. His letters are filled with examples of mutual
trust and support.

For a while, I avoided peers who were wiser and spiritually
stronger than me. I knew they'd challenge me and I'd feel inferior,
and my pride wouldn't let me get in those situations. Gradually,
though, I learned that I needed a mentor. Dave was—and is—
God's gift to me, and I'm grateful to have other spiritual coaches
as well. Athletes may be gifted, but they usually excel only under
the eye of a coach who draws out the best in them.

I've seen a lot of shallow connections among men, but I've
had the privilege to be involved in a few rich, real relationships.
Shared experiences in the military form strong bonds, and it's
no different in the church. We need vital connections with a
group of spiritually mature men. The list of possible activities is
almost endless: camping, hunting, fishing, Jiu Jitsu, mission trips,
building houses for Habitat for Humanity, specific and unique
service projects to meet a need of someone in the community,

volunteering together with partner organizations, and on and on. When we participate with other men, we see them outside of the church or Bible study context, and we get to know them in ways we simply can't if we're confined within walls.

I recently put a group of guys together, and we participated in an event created by David Goggins, one that tested everyone involved and allowed us to get to know each other at a much deeper level. It's called "The 4 x 4 x 48 Challenge." Six of us committed to run four miles every four hours over a forty-eight-hour weekend. Those who were crazy enough to sign up were my buddy Kyle; Kyle's eleven-year-old son Quinn; Gigi, my good friend and black belt coach; Jackson, a senior in high school at the time; my thirteen-year-old son Caleb; and me. I didn't expect Caleb to do all the runs, but he ran over twenty miles and biked much of the rest with Quinn. I was really proud of him. Over the weekend, all of us encountered stress and hit some kind of wall. Kyle and I were the only ones to finish all the runs, but that wasn't the point. In the grind of getting up in the middle of the night to run four miles in the cold and wind, and in our conversations on the road and back at the house where we stayed, we got to know each other far better than if we hadn't responded to the challenge and encouraged each other. On one of the runs with Kyle, he asked, "Hey, can we walk a little?"

I responded, "You bet." We walked together as brothers, supporting each other when we felt exhausted and vulnerable.

Kyle did something many of us refuse to do: he asked for help. We might not want to ask our pastor or another leader for help because we don't want to look weak or we don't want to waste the person's time. As my Rescue Swimmer training was about to end, we were on one of our long runs, and a guy who was barely running called out to me, "Hey, Bowen, I'm not sure I can make it. My knee is killing me. Would you help me?"

I told him, "Take my arm. I'll get you to the finish line. You haven't come all this way for nothing. We're going to do this together." Over the weeks before that run, he and I had eaten together, swum together, run together, thrown up together, and all the rest that training demands. In that moment, he could have given in to his pride and tried to go it alone, and I'm not sure he would have made it. Just telling me he needed some help and hearing my encouragement was all he needed. With me at his side, he limped and staggered across the finish line, but he made it. He qualified, and he'll always remember the last part of our last run. So will I.

Asking for help takes humility and courage, and helping others requires compassion, but let me offer a warning. It's not productive to try to help someone who doesn't want it. They may not take the initiative to ask, but whether they ask or we offer, they have to be willing to accept help. We don't do anyone any favors by forcing ourselves on them, unless, of course, it's a matter of life and death.

Resilience is a rare trait because it's not just gritting our teeth and hanging on. It's more than that. It's the willingness to look for God in the middle of our troubles, ask others for help, and trust that God is active behind the scenes even when we don't see His hand at work.

THINK ABOUT IT:

1. What are some ways difficulties reveal what's already present in our hearts? How have you seen this happen in others' lives? And in yours?

2. What are some signs Satan is a lion who is trying to devour someone?

3. Review 2 Corinthians 7:8-10 and the paragraphs about this passage. Before you read the section of the chapter about repentance, what was your view of it? What is it now? What, if anything, changed your perspective of repentance?

4. How is repentance like course corrections for an airplane or a ship? What does that tell you about the frequency of how we can (and should) practice repentance?

5. What are some reasons men don't want to be vulnerable? Which of those are valid, and which aren't?

6. How would a mentor or spiritual coach help you in your walk with Christ and your application of God's Word to every area of your life?

CHAPTER 8

The Tenacious

But in your hearts honor Christ the Lord as holy, always
being prepared to make a defense to anyone who asks
you for a reason for the hope that is in you; yet do it
with gentleness and respect.

—1 Peter 3:15

> If we have got the true love of God shed abroad in our
> hearts, we will show it in our lives. We will not have to
> go up and down the earth proclaiming it. We will show it
> in everything we say or do.
>
> —Dwight L. Moody

In the last chapter, we looked at the internal fight against
selfishness, and we saw the solution is repentance. In this chapter,
we'll see our *external* tension to be "in the world but not of the
world," and the solution is love.

Let me pick up on the point at the end of Chapter 6: I'm not
sure how it happened (there are many theories by theologians,
scholars, and sociologists), but many in the church today are
more passionate about protecting their rights than in following
Christ's example to love the unloved and the unlovely. The question I ask myself and others is simple: Where is your flag planted?
If it's planted in Jesus alone, your character will gradually conform

to His image, your heart will break with what breaks His, and your actions will reflect His kindness, courage, generosity, and patience—especially toward the vulnerable, the marginalized, the despised, and those who disagree with you. There are, to be sure, some whose lives reflect God's amazing grace, but as I look at people in the church today (and in the mirror), I see three main problems:

SOME ARE PASSIVE

Some people are just going through the motions in their walk of faith . . . so it's more of a walk of superficial commitment and a lack of passion. They're passive, maybe reading their Bibles and praying from time to time, but maybe not. Average church attendance has slipped in recent years from three Sundays in four, to two, and now less than two. So today, a person is considered a "regular church attender" by showing up twice a month, usually for an hour, and who knows how engaged or bored the person may be for that brief time? A recent study reports that "while the majority of Christians they interviewed don't belong to a local church, they still identify with their church roots. 'Never mind the fact that they attend church less than 12 times a year,' sociologist Penny Long Marler observes. 'We estimate that 78 million Protestants are in that place. Ask most pastors what percentage of inactive members they have—they'll say anything from 40 to 60 percent.'"[23]

Putting your rear end in a seat in church on Sunday morning doesn't guarantee a vibrant faith and bold, creative service. Instead, it often reflects only a lukewarm attitude toward God and His kingdom.

SOME ARE PREOCCUPIED

Yeah, I know. You're busy. So am I. A lot of people are pre-occupied with distractions that are, at best, secondary. They've devoted their lives to building a career, and they're exhausted on the weekends and want to sleep in, play golf, or do something other than worship on Sunday. But others are preoccupied for a different reason: they're genuinely overwhelmed by the problems in their lives. Sickness, a recent death in the family, divorce, a way-ward child, caring for elderly parents, crushing debt, and the ravages of different forms of abuse have eroded their energy, clouded their thinking, and left them hopeless. Their only thoughts about God are that He has let them down.

SOME ARE POSSESSED

We can be possessed by an intense desire for career advance-ment, wealth, advanced degrees, a bigger house, a nicer car, or anything else. Our hearts can focus on literally anything more than God, but I want to return to the topic of politics. As I men-tioned earlier, I've seen far more Christians express passion for a political leader than for Christ in the last few years. They feed their minds on news programs that enflame these white-hot emotions, and they discount any thought that challenges their thinking. This is called "confirmation bias"—people listen only to views they already believe, and they seek out sources that confirm their existing biases. Of course, this happens to people across the political spectrum, but I'm especially alarmed by those from the Christian, conservative right.

The Scriptures are full of admonitions for believers to follow God's example to care for outcasts, misfits, the unlovely, and those who are overlooked by society. Where is the passion for this clear calling? Instead, we see Christians (not all by any means, but far too many) who communicate with ferocity about keeping immigrants out of our country, defy any attempts to stem the epidemic of gun violence, stand against anyone proposing a living wage for those at the bottom of the economic ladder, and other hot button issues. No, I'm not a flaming liberal, and each of these issues (and many others) is very difficult to solve. I'm not recommending a liberal solution, just a biblical one.

I'm not recommending a liberal solution, just a biblical one.

We can advocate for secure borders *and* compassionate treatment for those who are fleeing oppression and seeking security for their families. We can support our brave and capable police *and* advocate changes in training to minimize senseless killings. We can advocate for a fair tax policy *and* reasonable spending policies. We can be pro-life *and* provide practical support for women who have trouble caring for a child. We can advocate for traditional gender roles and marriage *and* have empathy for those who live alternate lifestyles. These problems are incredibly complex. My purpose here isn't to lay out thorough solutions to intractable problems, but to point us to Jesus so that our words and faces communicate both grace *and* truth, not one or the other. If I believe that the people who disagree with me are evil fools, there's no way I'll love them well. But if I believe they are people created in the image of God, of inestimable value and deserving respect, I'll honor them with a listening ear and a humble heart. We'll still disagree, but I'll see them as people with hopes and dreams much like mine.

Some readers might respond, "Yeah, but wasn't Jesus angry sometimes? Doesn't that justify our political anger?" My answer is "yes" and "no." Jesus displayed anger, but not because His political convictions were challenged. In John 2, He went to the temple and saw that vendors had set up shop in God's sacred space, the place where heaven and earth met. His anger was directed at those who valued profits over God. Certainly, many others throughout Palestine also had misplaced passion for wealth, but these were set up in God's house, which was intended to be "a house of prayer." In John 11, Jesus trembled with anger and grief as He stood at the tomb of His friend Lazarus. This time, His anger was focused on the tragedy and injustice of death itself, which wasn't God's original plan for mankind. And in Mark 10, when the disciples tried to keep children away from Jesus, He became "indignant" because the disciples cared only about their power and prestige, not those who were habitually overlooked in their culture, like women and children.

Christian nationalism and insistence on rights aren't in the ballpark of the reasons Jesus got angry. In fact, I believe Jesus is angry and the Holy Spirit is grieved when believers are enraged over politics. Not convinced? When the religious leaders tried to trick Jesus by asking Him about taxes, they thought they had Him in a corner because if He said, "Don't pay taxes to Caesar," He would be an insurrectionist, but if He said, "Pay the taxes," He would be allied with the hated Romans. His response was nuanced and brilliant: "Render to Caesar the things that are Caesar's, and to God the things that are God's" (Mark 12:17). Those listening were stunned by His wisdom. He was saying, "The things of God sometimes overlap with human politics, but Christians must always put God's kingdom first." And His kingdom is full of both grace and truth—which means we need to value God's truth over political beliefs, and every word we say and every encounter with others should be marked by compassion, kindness, gentleness, and grace. That's not what I see on the faces or hear from the lips of many, many Christians today.

If our hearts are fixed on something or someone other than Jesus, we'll almost certainly become passive, preoccupied, or possessed by a passion that pulls us away from Him. I'm generally not known as a passive guy, but I can certainly be preoccupied or possessed. It usually happens around my business pursuits. In 2014, I realized that a New Jersey packaging business I owned actually owned me. I was far too preoccupied with the day-to-day responsibilities because I was possessed with a passion for success. I sensed the Lord wanted me to sell the company to free me up to move to a place more conducive to the spiritual and emotional health of our family . . . and selling it would enable me to pay off the debt my father left me.

Four years after I sold the company, my non-compete period was over, and a multinational packaging company in Europe contacted me about establishing a partnership to start another packaging company in Minnesota. At the time, I was growing a lot in my faith. Dave had become my mentor, our family attended River Valley Church, a large and vibrant church, and I was involved in our men's ministry. In many ways, it was a no-brainer: I knew the business inside and out, I wouldn't have to move our family, and the money was fantastic. As I held the contract in my hands and prayed, I sensed God ask me, "Will this draw you closer to Me or lead you farther away?" I tried to ignore Him because I was so excited about the opportunity. Sung knew this was going to be the wrong move for us, but she didn't say anything. She just prayed and trusted that God would clearly show me. Suddenly, God showed me the price I'd pay (and my family would pay) if I signed the contract, and at that moment, all the benefits and opportunities faded into the background. One thing was most important. I called the man and said, "Thank you for coming to see me and making this generous offer. I really appreciate it. You may not understand this, but I believe God is telling me not to move forward with this business opportunity. The responsibilities would have a detrimental impact on me and my family, so I need to decline."

You never know how business people might respond to a call like this. To my surprise (and relief), he was magnificent. He replied, "I'm glad you made the decision now instead of later. It's good for both of us to be clear from the beginning. It was wonderful to meet you and spend time with you. Good luck."

Was this a fantastic open door for me? No question. Did I want to do it? You bet. But I realized it wasn't going to prepare me to be at my best, to give my heart fully to God and be fully present with Sung and the children. I would have been preoccupied and possessed. Love is more important . . . far more important.

LOVE THEM ANYWAY

When Peter wrote his letters, his audience was vastly different from us. They had been run out of Palestine by ferocious persecution. They weren't just *spiritual* aliens in a pagan world; they were *literal* aliens seeking refuge from attacks. It would have been easy for them to play the role of victims... because they *were* victims! But Peter told them to be strong, to focus on the grace of God, and to let their light shine even when they were threatened and dispossessed. He wrote: "Now who is there to harm you if you are zealous for what is good? But even if you should suffer for righteousness' sake, you will be blessed. Have no fear of them, nor be troubled, but in your hearts honor Christ the Lord as holy, always being prepared to make a defense to anyone who asks you for a reason for the hope that is in you; yet do it with gentleness and respect, having a good conscience, so that, when you are slandered, those who revile your good behavior in Christ may be put to shame. For it is better to suffer for doing good, if that should be God's will, than for doing evil" (1 Peter 3:13-17).

In a hostile environment, tell people about Jesus, and tell them "with gentleness and respect." If that was the standard for people who were marginalized as refugees, what would it be for those of us who live in the most prosperous and free nation the world has ever known?

Did you catch that? In a hostile environment, tell people about Jesus, and tell them "with gentleness and respect." If that was the standard for people who were marginalized as refugees, what would it be for those of us who live in the most prosperous and free nation the world has ever known? Instead of complaining about everything we disagree about, maybe we could follow Jesus' example and Peter's admonition to love those who disagree with us, listen to them so well that we can articulate their positions as well as they can, and affirm that at least some of their points have some validity. (They do.)

We aren't going to win souls for eternity if those people have concluded that we hate them. Even if we disagree, we need to demonstrate genuine love for them. I sometimes use an exercise to gauge the depth of my love for people. 1 Corinthians 13 is often read at weddings, and people sigh because they assume it's so sweet . . . but that's not how the people first reading this passage would have responded! Paul was showing them how far they'd fallen short, and he was rebuking and correcting them. The Corinthian Christians were arrogant and petty. They fought about all kinds of things instead of loving each other. That's the background of this chapter. Paul pointed out the wrong things they were boasting in—their spiritual gifts, their power, and their manipulative generosity. Those were all worthless because they weren't propelled by love. He drove the spur into them:

> If I speak in the tongues of men and of angels, but have not love, I am a noisy gong or a clanging cymbal. And if I have prophetic powers, and understand all mysteries and all knowledge, and if I have all faith, so as to remove mountains, but have not love, I am nothing. If I give away all I

have, and if I deliver up my body to be burned, but have not love, I gain nothing. (1 Corinthians 13:1-3)

In other words, it doesn't matter how right you are, how passionate you are about a political leader or party, how much you sacrifice and give, or any other way you try to dominate or intimidate others to get your way. If you don't truly love them, you've missed it all. In Paul's language, you're just making noise, you are nothing, and you gain nothing. Quite an indictment!

When I look at the next part of the passage, I put my name in it to test myself and see how much I'm genuinely loving Sung, the kids, my friends, the people I work with, our neighbors, the people of our church, those who agree with me, and those who don't:

- Is Michael patient and kind?
- Does Michael envy or boast?
- Is Michael arrogant or rude?
- Does Michael insist on his own way?
- Is Michael irritable or resentful?
- Does Michael rejoice at wrongdoing, or does he rejoice with the truth?
- Does Michael bear all things, believe all things, hope all things, endure all things?

When I finish this exercise, I never think, *Hey, I've got this! Slam dunk.* No, people's faces flash in my mind as I recall times when I failed to love like Jesus. It's sobering, and it's necessary.

In our family, we make a list of expectations for each of us every week. For a while, the list focused only on the chores, but we realized we needed to include expressing love, respect, and kindness as top priorities for each of us every week. To Paul, loving people in a way that they knew they were loved wasn't negotiable.

We can't manufacture these qualities of love. They have to overflow from a deep well of love we experience. When we read the Bible, pray, worship, and spend time with believers, our goal isn't to fill up an hour or so. God's purpose for these things is to draw us close, convince us of our need for grace and His abundant provision, and fill us to the point of overflowing. As we've seen, we need to be sure to get the order right. Our love for God is stimulated by our experience of His love for us. He takes the initiative. We'll only make Him our treasure if we realize He considers us to be His treasure.

The experience of God's love (or the lack of this experience) shapes our attitudes and actions toward all people, especially those who aren't like us. In the time of Jesus and Paul, Jews and Gentiles were like the left and right political world for us today—they hated each other, were suspicious of each other, and were sure the other side was evil. Gentiles who had found God could come to the temple in Jerusalem, but they had to stay behind a wall that kept them from worshiping with the Jews. The gospel changed everything. Both ethnic groups are equal in the family of God. It was just as shocking to one group as the other. Paul explained:

> But now in Christ Jesus you who once were far off have been brought near by the blood of Christ. For he himself is our peace, who has made us both one and has broken down in his flesh the dividing wall of hostility by abolishing the law of commandments expressed in

ordinances, that he might create in himself one new man in place of the two, so making peace, and might reconcile us both to God in one body through the cross, thereby killing the hostility. And he came and preached peace to you who were far off and peace to those who were near. For through him we both have access in one Spirit to the Father. So then you are no longer strangers and aliens, but you are fellow citizens with the saints and members of the household of God. (Ephesians 2:13-19)

Jesus' death on the cross obliterated the dividing wall and killed the hatred that kept people apart. (I love the power and finality in Paul's language.) That means that people who are believers who look different, speak a different language, and hold different views are our brothers and sisters in Christ—and we treat them with the utmost respect and kindness.

But what about "those people," the ones who are different from us and don't claim to know God? We're to love them, too. Who were "those people" in the first century in Palestine? The Samaritans and the Romans. The Jews hated both groups. The Samaritans were of mixed race, the descendants of Jews who returned after the Babylonian exile and Gentiles, and the Romans were the iron fist that had conquered the Holy Land and demanded taxes to pay for the soldiers posted there. It was entirely normal to despise both groups, but Jesus had a different solution:

"You have heard that it was said, 'You shall love your neighbor and hate your enemy.' But I say to you, Love your enemies and pray for those who persecute you, so that you may be sons of your Father who is in heaven. For he makes his sun rise on the evil and on the good, and sends rain on the just and on the unjust. For if you love those who love you, what reward do you have? Do not even the tax collectors do the same? And if you greet only your brothers, what more are you doing than others? Do not even the Gentiles do the same? You therefore must be perfect, as your heavenly Father is perfect." (Matthew 5:43-48)

Later in Matthew's account of the life of Christ, the Pharisees again tried to catch Jesus off guard so they could mock Him. One of them asked Him, "Teacher, which is the great commandment in the Law?" (Matthew 22:36)

It was common among the law-abiding religious leaders to discuss this question, and whichever one Jesus picked, they were ready to pounce. But Jesus gave an irrefutable answer: "You shall love the Lord your God with all your heart and with all your soul and with all your mind. This is the great and first commandment. And a second is like it: You shall love your neighbor as yourself. On these two commandments depend all the Law and the Prophets" (vv. 37-40).

Our "neighbor," Jesus explained, isn't a narrow, exclusive category. It includes everybody. Yes, everybody.

Our "neighbor," Jesus explained, isn't a narrow, exclusive category. It includes everybody. Yes, everybody. Do you think people around you who are of a different ethnic background, socioeconomic level, language, and outlook believe you truly love them? I hope so.

My faith and my walk are like the stock market: sometimes up, sometimes down, but generally trending upward. I'd like to say that I love like Jesus, but I certainly can't say that. But I can say that I love people more like Jesus loves them today than I did ten years ago, five years ago, and a year ago, and I'll take progress every time. This is part of the tension we experience as we follow Jesus: we'd rather be exclusive, but the Holy Spirit prompts us to be inclusive; we'd rather see ourselves as victims and wallow in self-pity and resentment, but Jesus sees us as overcomers who are indwelt by the Holy Spirit with love for every person.

LOVE IN ACTION

Years ago, a popular worship song said, "They'll know we are Christians by our love." That has been true since the foundation of the church in the first century, and it's true today. When believers have loved well, lives have been changed and the world sat up and noticed. Throughout the ages, the church founded hospitals and orphanages, led the fight against slavery, advocated for fair wages and better working conditions, cared for unwed mothers, provided job training, and fed millions who were hungry—and we're still involved in many of those ways. These acts of love are remarkable, but there has been, perhaps, no better example of love in action than the believers' response to two devastating plagues in the Roman Empire in the second and third centuries. The first one was probably smallpox, and the second may have been measles. Both times, about one fourth of the entire population of the empire died.[24] Those plagues made COVID-19 look like a stumped toe.

During those plagues, most of the doctors fled from the cities to save their own lives, and many pagans left their family members who had gotten sick. Without basic care of food and water, most of them died, but the Christians stepped in to care for their own who were sick . . . and the pagans, too. Dionysius, bishop of Alexandria, reported:

> Most of our brother Christians showed unbounded love and loyalty, never sparing themselves and thinking only of one another. Heedless of danger, they took charge of the sick, attending to their every need and ministering to them in Christ, and with them departed this life serenely happy; for they were infected by others with the disease, drawing on themselves the sickness of their neighbors and cheerfully accepting their pains. Many, in nursing and curing others, transferred their death to themselves and died in their stead.

The self-sacrifice of the Christians stood in stark contrast to the self-protection of the pagans. Dionysius described the contrast:

> But with the heathen everything was quite otherwise. They deserted those who began to be sick, and fled from their dearest friends. They shunned any participation or fellowship with death; which yet, with all their precautions, it was not easy for them to escape.[25]

Writing for the Gospel Coalition, Glen Scrivener observes:

The third-century plague found in the church a Spirit-filled people, willing to walk the way of their Master. Plagues intensify the natural course of life. They intensify our own sense of mortality and frailty. They also intensify opportunities to display countercultural, counterconditional love.

Christian death rates were significantly lower than those of the general population (perhaps only 10 percent, though the word "only" is a fearful qualifier). The mutual love of brothers and sisters in Christ meant that, on the one hand, those who provided care were at a higher risk of infection, but on the other, those who were infected had better survival rates. As these Christians made themselves vulnerable to death, they actually found life. Once the plague had swept through, Christians were stronger. They were stronger as a proportion of society, since more of them survived. They had more resilience because they had a robust hope in the face of death. And they were stronger as communities, forging even closer bonds through the sufferings they'd faced.[26]

At the beginning of the first plague in 165 a.d., the Christian church was a small, marginalized sect, less than one-tenth of one percent of the population of the Roman Empire, but after the love displayed by believers in the two devastating plagues, the church grew to over half of the empire's population by 350.[27] How did this explosion of conversions happen? Love in action, pure and simple.

Jesus lived in the tension of being in the world but not of the world, and He has called each of us to live in that tension, too. It's not easy. It's much easier to deny the tension exists and gravitate to one side or the other: being so spiritual that we're oblivious to the needs and passions of the people in the world . . . or more likely, getting so caught up in the passions of politics and economics that we don't even try to live for Christ there (or we claim that *is* living for Christ).

CHOOSE YOUR FRIENDS WISELY

King Solomon told us, "Whoever walks with the wise becomes wise, but the companion of fools will suffer harm" (Proverbs 13:20). We often tell our kids to choose their friends carefully because who they hang out with shapes their future. We need to give ourselves the same advice, because our friends shape our future, too. Rescue Swimmers are part of a chosen, well-trained, experienced team united around the same cause. Whether we dropped from a helicopter or jumped off the deck of a destroyer, we worked together to accomplish a common purpose: to save the life of a pilot and the crew. Those who have ever been on a team like this—in the military or anywhere else—know the power of a cohesive, well-oiled, mutually supportive team. I believe that's what God wants for all of us. We don't have Rescue Swimmer or SEAL training to forge these bonds, so we need to create environments where we can walk with the wise and absorb their passion for Christ and their wisdom to live well.

It's really challenging to live in the tension between two kingdoms. I can take the easy way out like anyone else, but I'll suffer for it. Even more, the kingdom suffers when I don't make regular corrections to keep the ship of my life on course, and it suffers when I'm passive, preoccupied, or possessed by anything other than Jesus. When that happens, my light flickers and my salt loses its flavor.

I don't just enjoy hanging out with Dave and the other men who love me well . . . I desperately need them! I need their godly example, their kind hearts, their fierce loyalty, their humor, and their willingness to say hard things to me when I need to hear them. They aren't the least bit surprised when I tell them I'm having a hard time figuring out how to live in the tension between two kingdoms, and they aren't the least bit hesitant to give me a hand to help me take the next step of faith.

THINK ABOUT IT:

1. Describe what it means to live in the tension between two kingdoms, to be "in the world but not of the world."

2. Why does being passive look attractive to some men? What's the cost?

3. Why is it so easy to be preoccupied and distracted from the heart and the purposes of God? What's the price we pay for that?

4. How would you explain the energy and passion behind being possessed by career advancement, wealth, education, and possessions? And how would you explain the reason Christians can be possessed by politics, the news media, and people who disagree with us? How does that affect our walks with God, our emotional health, and our relationships with those who don't agree with us?

5. When you need to make a significant decision, how would it help you to ask yourself, "Will this pull me closer to Christ or lead me farther away from Him?"

6. Look again at Ephesians 2:13-19. What are some specific steps to help you take down barriers and "kill the hatred" we see in our country?

7. We hear believers talk a lot about their rights today. What would the Christians who loved pagans during the plagues say to us about rights?

8. Describe the impact you're having on your friends. Describe the impact they have on you.

CHAPTER 9

The Disciplined

For the moment all discipline seems painful rather than pleasant, but later it yields the peaceful fruit of righteousness to those who have been trained by it.

—Hebrews 12:11

NO MORE. No more excuses. No more: "I'll start tomorrow." No more: "Just this once." No more accepting the shortfalls of my own will. No more taking the easy road. No more bowing down to whatever unhealthy or unproductive thoughts float through my mind.

—Jocko Willink

Soon after I had come clean with Sung, we were both emotionally spent and needed time to process all that I had shared. I rented a beach house about five blocks from our home in St. Augustine so I could be alone, spend time with God, experience His love and kindness, and pray things out. For months, I'd been meeting with some men who practiced meditation—not Eastern mysticism, but dwelling on God's Word so intently that it sinks into a person's soul. They talked about quieting their minds before the Lord so He could fill them with His truth, His love, and His directions. From their description of this practice, I could tell it wasn't just reading and praying. It was more intense, more life-giving . . .

and more demanding. I met with them during my time away at the beach house, and one of the men told me, "I spend between eight and fifteen minutes when I meditate. Michael, I can't begin to tell you what it has meant to my walk with God. You should try it. I have to warn you, though, that most people can't get beyond the first couple of minutes before they're distracted."

I took it as a personal challenge. I wasn't going to get distracted. I was determined to out-meditate that guy. In fact, I was going to take meditation to a whole new level with God! In that conversation, Rod, an older member of the group who was Irish, a mountain of a man with a take-no-prisoners approach to life, weighed in on the topic of meditation. When I shared my struggles and my recent breakthrough with the group, Rod opened his Bible and read James 1:2-8:

> Count it all joy, my brothers, when you meet trials of various kinds, for you know that the testing of your faith produces steadfastness. And let steadfastness have its full effect, that you may be perfect and complete, lacking in nothing.
>
> If any of you lacks wisdom, let him ask God, who gives generously to all without reproach, and it will be given him. But let him ask in faith, with no doubting, for the one who doubts is like a wave of the sea that is driven and tossed by the wind. For that person must not suppose that he will receive anything from the Lord; he is a double-minded man, unstable in all his ways.

He said, "I want you to memorize at least the first part of this passage and meditate on it."

I answered, "I'll do it. In fact, I'll do it tomorrow morning."

I got up at 4:45 and walked toward the beach. The moon and the stars were blazing in the sky. It was a perfect morning—I could hear the waves hitting the shore, and I smelled the salt air; it was about 72 degrees. As I walked on a boardwalk over the dunes to the beach, I saw something in the distance at the end of the boardwalk. I assumed it was someone who had beaten me to the spot, but as I got closer, I could tell it was a folding beach chair someone had left there. I picked up the chair and took it out to the sand. I set the timer on my phone for eight minutes, and I began meditating on the first part of the James passage. I was all set for "the meditation challenge." I tapped "start," and launched into my first endeavor to meditate. I went over the second verse, and I went over it again. I then focused on each word, and I repeated the process. At that point, I began to feel a bit antsy. I thought, *Oh man, I've been doing this so long. Surely the timer is ready to go off!* I looked at the timer. I still had five minutes and two seconds to go! I was so frustrated! I put the phone down and determined, through clenched teeth, to keep meditating until it went off. I'm not sure that's exactly an attitude that's conducive to getting in touch with God, but that's what happened that morning.

After the eight minutes were over, I took a walk down the beach. During the walk, the sun came up over the ocean. The sky was beautiful—it was a glorious morning. As I walked back, I saw things I'd missed when I began in the dark. I noticed a single chair sitting in the sand down from a boardwalk. It had been my haven an hour or so earlier. As I stepped onto the boardwalk, I noticed a blue rock with the word "Joy" painted on it. That was exactly the message in the first verse of my passage in James: "Count it all joy." No one knew I was there that morning, and the only person who knew I was meditating on James 1:2 was Rod, and I was sure he hadn't put it there—not exactly his MO. It turns out that some people paint rocks with single words and put them where they will be seen at parks, beaches, and wherever people go for recreation. This one was just for me. I'm convinced God led that tenderhearted person to put it right there right then. I call it my "joy rock," and I still have it.

> My sins had been robbing me of my joy, but I saw this rock as God's personal encouragement to me. Since then, I've joined the conspiracy of love.

My sins had been robbing me of my joy, but I saw this rock as God's personal encouragement to me. Since then, I've joined the conspiracy of love. I paint rocks blue and write "joy," "hope," and "love" on them, and I trust God will use at least one of them (and hopefully many more) to touch someone's heart the way the joy rock touched mine. I carry them with me, and when I feel led, I look around to see that nobody is watching, and I leave one on a stump, a bench, a table, a railing, or some other spot where people will walk by and see it. I'm paying the encouragement forward.

TWO SIDES OF DISCIPLINE

It has become "the D word." We live in such a self-indulgent culture that many of us are sure life should be easy, fun, and meaningful . . . with no effort on our part. That's a pipedream. There are actually two kinds of discipline, and we need to practice both of them if we're going to experience all God wants for us.

The first kind is corrective. We talk about disciplining our kids when they get out of line, and we argue with our spouse about the best way to do it. The point behind all the negotiations is that misbehavior must have some kind of consequences so the child realizes there's a price to pay for disobedience or a sour attitude. But discipline isn't just for our kids. We need it too. It can come as a not-too-favorable performance review and an imposed SOP, standard of performance. Or it can come from the loving hand of God. The writer to the Hebrews explains:

> And have you forgotten the exhortation that addresses you as sons?
>
> "My son, do not regard lightly the discipline of the Lord,
>   nor be weary when reproved by him.
> For the Lord disciplines the one he loves,
>   and chastises every son whom he receives."
>
> It is for discipline that you have to endure. God is treating you as sons. For what son is there whom his father does not discipline? If you are left without discipline, in which all have participated, then you are illegitimate children and not sons. Besides this, we have had earthly fathers who disciplined us and we respected them. Shall we not much more be subject to the Father of spirits and live? For they disciplined us for a short time as it seemed best to them, but he disciplines us for our good, that we may share his holiness. (Hebrews 12:5-10)

When we use the word "discipline," traumatic memories are triggered in the minds of some of us because our fathers didn't discipline us the way the Hebrews writer is talking about. It sure didn't feel like they were doing it for our good! It wasn't restorative; it was terrifying. As we saw earlier, some of us have the privilege of comparing God's nature to our loving, strong parents and how they treated us, but many of us have to do the hard but necessary work to contrast God with our parents, especially our dads. If the word *discipline* brings up painful memories and makes you recoil, you probably have some work to do to grieve the loss of love and safety, forgive your parents for the harm they've done to you, and experience God's healing love. Know this: God never disciplines in anger. It's always and only out of pure love—to draw you close, not to terrify you, and to build you up, not to crush you into submission. If we sense His heart for us in the discipline, we'll thank Him for it instead of despising it. Yeah, I know, that's not our first response, but we need to feast our hearts on God's love so we'll see His correction as an act of pure grace.

Know this: God never disciplines in anger. It's always and only out of pure love—to draw you close, not to terrify you, and to build you up, not to crush you into submission.

God disciplines (or corrects) us in many different ways. He may use His Word to point out where we're off track so we'll repent; He may use a spouse or mentor or someone else to call us to account for our behavior that falls short of God's love and integrity; His Spirit may whisper to us that a change is necessary; painful circumstances from out of nowhere may cause us to sit up and take notice, or most often, the painful circumstances are the clear consequences of our dumb choices.

The second kind of discipline isn't corrective; it's instructive, and it's designed to maximize our freedom . . . but always at a price. For instance:

- If we want the freedom of good health, we need to pay the price of exercise, eating right, and getting adequate sleep.

- If we want to enjoy financial freedom, we don't have to be rich, but we want to have enough that we're not worried about having enough. This freedom comes from the discipline of limiting our spending to less than our income, saving, investing, and giving—and of course, getting out of debt.

- If we want relational freedom, we need to resolve nagging misunderstandings and conflicts. This freedom comes from living in the blend of truth and love. If someone knows the truth about you but doesn't love you, it's scary. If someone loves you but doesn't really know you, it's superficial. But when someone knows us well and loves us deeply—and we love them the same way—we find real joy in the relationship.

- If we want to have the freedom to choose our career path, where we work and how we work, we need to pay the price of investing in training and mentoring.

In the opening of this chapter, I quote Jocko Willink's book, *Discipline Equals Freedom*. I love that quote and the lessons he teaches in the book, but I'd add an insight from the apostle Paul: "Rather train yourself for godliness; for while bodily training is of some value, godliness is of value in every way, as it holds promise for the present life and also for the life to come" (1 Timothy 4:7-8). In other words: godly discipline equals spiritual freedom.

Godly discipline equals spiritual freedom.

The most cherished goal is spiritual freedom. In his letter to the Galatians, Paul told them, "For freedom Christ has set us free; stand firm therefore, and do not submit again to a yoke of slavery" (Galatians 5:1). They had lived bound by the chains of trying to earn God's acceptance by keeping rigid rules—and they completely missed the heart of God. They tried to pay the price of spiritual freedom themselves, but it doesn't happen that way. We don't pay the price. Jesus has already paid it. Jesus' last word on the cross was *tetelestai,* which in Greek means "paid in full."

In his letter to the Colossians, Paul uses the metaphor of a debtors' prison. Our sins are the debts that were the reason for our imprisonment, and we had no way to pay them. The jailor was Satan. Paul explained that Jesus canceled "the record of debt that stood against us with its legal demands. This he set aside, nailing it to the cross. He disarmed the rulers and authorities and put them to open shame, by triumphing over them in him" (Colossians

2:14-15). Our debt wasn't excused, and it wasn't reduced to "time served." It had to be paid in full, and it required more than we could ever afford. In that day, a scroll listing the person's debts was nailed to the cell door. Jesus took our scrolls and nailed them to the cross—his cell—where He paid our debts and defeated the jailer. We're free. Grace is completely free to us, but it cost Jesus everything.

I've known people who were tremendously disciplined in one area but neglected others. Some athletes devote their lives to be at the top level of their sport, but sometimes they don't focus enough on their families or finances or spirituality or some other aspect of life. Godly discipline is balanced, giving us the security we need to avoid being obsessive-compulsive about a particular goal, and giving us the wisdom we need to pursue each area of our lives. But "balance" doesn't imply that we mark off our days into equal blocks of time for each priority; it means we give the right amounts of time and attention to each one, and we flex when we need to, so we can experience freedom and joy.

Plenty of books describe how to make a goal into a habit. Let me just say that this process requires us to be targeted, intentional, and determined. We need to focus on a few goals at a time. Having pages of goals might impress someone, but it's a fool's errand—they're not going to happen. I'd suggest you have one in each area. When those become habits, set others. We need to be intentional, thinking about the benefits to keep us motivated and realizing our choices matter to those closest to us. And we need to be determined. Every significant goal comes with a price tag. At times we fail, we drift, we get tired . . . and we want to quit. It happens to all of us. One of the marks of maturity is self-control, in this case, sticking with the program during the grind so we can enjoy the glory in the future.

One of the marks of maturity is self-control, in this case, sticking with the program during the grind so we can enjoy the glory in the future.

GROWING IN GRACE

For centuries, believers who were serious about their faith have practiced "spiritual disciplines." They might include different practices, but most people recognize these: Bible reading, prayer, meditation, fasting, worship, fellowship with other believers, generosity, and service. If we're not careful, these can become measuring sticks of our spirituality, so people feel proud when they do them and ashamed when they don't. But spiritual disciplines aren't measuring sticks; they're stepping-stones to bring us closer to God in humility, sacrifice, and gratitude.

For instance, we don't read the Scriptures to check it off our list or impress someone. When we open the Bible, we say, "Lord, speak to me. I'm listening." And we listen for His Spirit to apply the message of a passage to our lives. In the same way, when we pray, we don't do it to earn points with God or make someone notice us. After all, Jesus warned, "And when you pray, you must not be like the hypocrites. For they love to stand and pray in the synagogues and at the street corners, that they may be seen by others. Truly, I say to you, they have received their reward. But when you pray, go into your room and shut the door and pray to your Father who is in secret. And your Father who sees in secret will reward you" (Matthew 6:5-6).

The motivation is the same for all the rest. We engage in these disciplines to know God better and make more of a difference in the lives of others. In his book about spiritual disciplines called *The Life You've Always Wanted*, pastor John Ortberg writes, "But to grow spiritually means to live increasingly as Jesus would in our unique place—to perceive what Jesus would perceive if he looked through our eyes, to think what he would think, to feel what he would feel, and therefore to do what he would do."[28]

Some people think that carving time out of their schedule for the spiritual disciplines is a waste of time—for them, it's a verse or two, a quick prayer, and out the door. That's preparation for sure . . . preparation for being in a spiritual coma!

REPETITION

Why do you think we have four Gospels? Why do you think Paul describes the wonder of grace in every letter he wrote? Why do you think Jesus told the disciples over and over again that He was going to be betrayed, condemned, and executed, but He'd rise on the third day? The answer is that "repetition aids learning," and in fact, without repetition, we seldom learn anything at all. Some people think that carving time out of their schedule for the spiritual disciplines is a waste of time—for them, it's a verse or two, a quick prayer, and out the door. That's preparation for sure . . . preparation for being in a spiritual coma!

Habits matter. They prepare us for every eventuality. Rob O'Neill chronicles his experiences as a SEAL in his book, The Operator, Firing the Shots That Killed Osama Bin Laden and My Years as a SEAL Team Warrior. He executed more than 400 missions, including Operation Red Wing (described in Marcus Lutrell's book and movie, Lone Survivor) and the rescue of Captain Phillips, who was held hostage by Somali pirates on his ship on the Indian Ocean. O'Neill is best known, however, as the SEAL who put three bullets in Osama Bin Laden in Abbottabad, Pakistan. The real story, the part that is sometimes overlooked, is the team's preparation for the raid. After the compound was identified as a 50-50 chance of being the home of Bin Laden, the team didn't just fly in and hope for the best. An exact replica of the compound was built in North Carolina, and SEAL Team 6 went through every conceivable scenario again and again. In combat, the unexpected always happens, but the team wanted to minimize surprises. In the first seconds of the actual raid, one of the stealth helicopters crashed. It could have been a disaster, but when O'Neill was asked about it, he deadpanned, "We planned on that."

In every field and every endeavor, preparation produces confidence, calm, and excellence. Discipline prepares us to be ready, respond wisely, and remain calm when a wrench is thrown into the gears. We're going to suffer setbacks, we're going to make some bad choices, and other people are going to let us down. If we're not prepared, those events will throw us for a loop. If we're prepared, we take the blow, make the necessary adjustments, and get back into the fight. It might look like this:

- We think ahead about our health before we go to the grocery store or sit down at the restaurant; we set our alarm and take the time to meet a friend at the gym; and we turn off the movie and go to bed so we can get enough sleep.

- We think ahead about our finances so we don't make snap (and dumb) decisions to spend money we don't have on things we don't need.

- We think ahead about what we want our careers to look like ten or twenty years later, and we acquire the education, training, and credentials we need to get there.

- And we think ahead about establishing patterns in our lives that draw us closer to God and make us more useful in His kingdom.

No, you may not be a Navy SEAL, but preparation is just as important for you as it is for them. One more thing: discipline in these areas makes you ready for more than you imagined. If you haven't run a mile in the last ten years but you decide you'd like to run a marathon, you can do it, but only by working on your stamina and technique. When we're regularly engaged in preparing ourselves, our goals get bigger—sometimes incrementally and sometimes in a burst of a new vision.

Growth in all these areas isn't like a helicopter ride to the top of a mountain. It's more like a long hike up the mountain, with blisters and beautiful overlooks, exhaustion and exhilaration. If we expect good health, strong finances, a great career, meaningful connections with people, and a vibrant spiritual life to be easy and quick, we'll inevitably be disappointed, and we'll give up pretty quickly. Be realistic and pay the price. It's worth it. Rob O'Neill challenges us:

In my experience, the one category of people who get reliably crushed in BUD/S are that noble demographic, the loudmouths. They're usually the first to ring the bell. As for who will make it, all I can say is: Are you the person who can convince your body that it can do anything you ask it to? Who can hit the wall and say, "What wall?" That strength of mind isn't associated with any ethnicity or level of skin pigmentation. It's not a function of size or musculature or IQ. In the end, it's sheer cussedness, and I'm guessing you're either born that way or you never get there.[29]

We may not have been "born that way," but we're born again that way. The good news is that Christians have something even SEALs may not have: the Holy Spirit's power to transform us from the inside out. The "sheer cussedness" required to be a SEAL is the opposite of the brokenness required to tap into the Spirit's limitless resources. As we pursue God, the Spirit produces the qualities of Jesus in us. Paul described it this way: "For you were called to freedom, brothers. Only do not use your freedom as an opportunity for the flesh, but through love serve one another. . . . But the fruit of the Spirit is love, joy, peace, patience, kindness, goodness, faithfulness, gentleness, self-control; against such things there is no law. And those who belong to Christ Jesus have crucified the flesh with its passions and desires" (Galatians 5:13, 22-24). "Crucifying the flesh" isn't something that happens once and it's over. It's something we do all day every day to say "no" to our selfish desires so we can say "yes" to the Spirit working in and through us.

In *Extreme Ownership*, Jocko Willink admits that sometimes he didn't want to get out of bed in the morning, so he set three alarms to force himself to get moving. He was willing to do anything to be a good leader. Crucifying the flesh isn't fun. It's a lot easier to coast, to give in to selfish desires, and gradually (or rapidly) drift away from God and His purposes. Thankfully, the Spirit whispers and shouts to get our attention and call us back to a life that's worth living.

SEALs don't train and fight as individuals but as small, cohesive teams. That's the way Christians grow, serve, and make a dent in our world: we have "iron sharpening iron" connections with other men. We live in a very individualistic culture, so we have to work harder to create and deepen those connections, but they've been important through all generations of believers . . . and they always include the spiritual disciplines. In Luke's account of the early church in Acts, he makes a simple observation about the quality of the relationships among the first believers: "And they devoted themselves to the apostles' teaching and the fellowship, to the breaking of bread and the prayers" (Acts 2:42). Are we devoted to these practices in relationships that shape us into Christ's likeness? Or is it too much trouble?

Both kinds of discipline—corrective and instructive—lead to freedom.

Last Christmas, someone sent me a link to a commercial that had gone viral. An old man sees a Christmas tree being brought into a home, and he has an idea. He rustles through a storage shed and finds a rusted kettlebell. He tries to lift it, but he can barely get it off the floor. The next scene is of an alarm going off early in the morning, and he struggles out of bed, gets up, and lifts the kettlebell a little higher. He groans with each attempt, making the neighbors curious or annoyed. Still, his regimen doesn't waver: day after day, the alarm and the exercise. Sometimes he looks in the mirror with an expression that says, "I don't know if I can do this," but he keeps going. One day, he's able to lift the weight to his shoulders . . . and then over his head. One of the neighbors calls his daughter to tell her the old man has lost his mind. When she comes to check on him, he keeps lifting. She has no idea what has gotten into him. On Christmas day, he shaves and puts on his best clothes, picks up a carefully wrapped present, and goes to his daughter's house. She gives him a hug. He turns and sees his little granddaughter coming down the stairs. He gives her the present—it's a star for the tree. As she holds it in her hands, he lifts her up so she can put it on the treetop. He smiles the biggest grandfather smile, and his daughter tears up in thankfulness and understanding.

That's a beautiful picture of the payoff of discipline. Don't miss it.

THINK ABOUT IT:

1. How would you define and differentiate between the two types of discipline?

2. Does the description of corrective discipline bring up any painful memories? If so, what will the healing process look like for you? Are you willing to go through it? Explain your answer.

3. Give yourself a grade. On a scale of 0 (nada) to 10 (champ), how disciplined are you in these areas:

___ Physical health (exercise, eating well, sleeping enough)

___ Financial security (limited spending, saving, investing, giving, getting out of debt)

___ Meaningful relationships (knowing and loving)

___ Your career (goals and aspirations)

___ Spiritual life

4. What does this exercise tell you?

5. What has been your attitude toward spiritual disciplines? What's your experience in practicing them? What's your next step in using them to stimulate your love for God and your desire to serve Him?

6. What are some reasons it's important to see spiritual growth as a long hike up a mountain instead of a helicopter ride to the top?

7. Look again at Galatians 5:13, 22-24. Describe what it means to "crucify the flesh." What does that mean in daily practice? What are the upsides of doing it?

8. What is one goal you can set in each of the areas of discipline? What's your specific plan (steps, times, midpoint goals, etc.) to reach them?

9. Which payoffs of discipline are most attractive to you?

CHAPTER 10

The Victorious

But thanks be to God, who in Christ always leads us in triumphal procession, and through us spreads the fragrance of the knowledge of him everywhere.

—2 Corinthians 2:14

> Return to the battle again, no longer trusting in the false and insufficient human resources which so foolishly we had taken into the battle, but now trusting in the limitless resources of our risen Lord.
>
> —Alan Redpath

It may seem strange for an ex-military guy to conclude a book with a story of a conscientious objector, but the story of *Hacksaw Ridge* describes a very different—and very profound—kind of personal victory. Corporal Desmond T. Doss wasn't a Navy SEAL, a Green Beret, or any other kind of usual military hero. He was a conscientious objector, one of only a handful who was awarded the Medal of Honor.

Doss joined the Army only a few months after the attack on Pearl Harbor, but his religious affiliation prevented him from carrying a weapon. Still, he wanted to serve his country. In boot camp, he endured unending harassment from the sergeant and the recruits. They tried to force him to go against his beliefs and be like them, but he steadfastly refused. They assumed he was a coward, but he was anything but. He became a combat medic, throwing himself into danger to care for wounded soldiers in the heat of battle. The movie depicts his courage in the Battle of Okinawa in May of 1945.

The battle is legendary for its ferocity. The Japanese were ready to defend their homeland to the last man, woman, and child, and this island was their proving ground to show the Allies the steep cost of an invasion. During the height of the battle, Doss repeatedly exposed himself to enemy fire to bandage wounds and carry or drag men to cover. He lowered each one down a cliff (the ridge in the title) by a rope, and then he went back into the carnage for another wounded soldier. Over these perilous hours, Doss rescued seventy-five men. The citation for the Medal of Honor describes this and other instances in the following weeks when he ignored his own safety to care for others. Eventually, he was hit with shrapnel and broke his arm. Instead of letting another medic help him, he tended to his own injuries so the medic could give attention to other soldiers.

When President Truman awarded the Medal, Doss wouldn't allow anyone in his hometown to publicize his heroic deeds. He was as humble as he was courageous. His faith caused him to be very different from the other men in his unit. He was a source of ridicule . . . until the other men realized he was willing to give his life for them.

This, I believe, is a wonderful example of a victorious Christian life. In his book, *The Making of a Man of God*, British evangelist, pastor, and author Alan Redpath identifies how this victory happens: "Let a man be right with God, reconciled

through the blood of the cross, humbled at the foot of Calvary;
let him be broken, coming to God guilty and hopeless and needy;
and at that moment God takes hold of him and transforms and
uses all his gifts and qualities, until that man becomes a mighty
influence. But he has first to come down from his ladder of pride
to the very foot of the cross."[30]

That's the story of Desmond Doss, and it can be ours, too.

RESILIENCE AND TENACITY

Another book by Alan Redpath has made a big impact on me.
In *Victorious Christian Living,* he inspires and challenges us:

> How easily does the child of God rest satisfied with
> past achievements! What a tragedy that is, for not only
> does he rob himself of the blessing of God, but he hinders
> other people and encourages Satan. No Christian will win
> the race if he stops to take a breather. No one will win the
> war if, on the very verge of victory, he asks for a furlough.
> No child of God can afford to take one minute's vacation
> from walking with God. How sad that so many of us have
> the prize almost within our grasp, the goal almost within
> reach, only to discover that we have come short of it and
> of the victory that could have been ours in Jesus Christ!
> We lost simply because we did not press home to possess
> what God had for us. We were overcome by inertia.[31]

Did you get that? "No Christian will win the race if he stops
to take a breather. No one will win the war if, on the very verge
of victory, he asks for a furlough." From time to time, all of us

are tempted to bail out on God's will. Sometimes, following Jesus seems just too hard, but quite often, we quit because His will doesn't line up with ours. (We've got it backward.) To put it simply, we feel the temptation to quit when we're discouraged, coast when we're bored, and rebel when we're angry. It's not a sin to *be* tempted; it's sin to *give in* to the temptation. Resilience is necessary for us to walk with God for a lifetime. And after we've failed (and we will, quite often), we need tenacity to repent, step back into the stream of God's purpose for us, and take the next step forward.

> To put it simply, we feel the temptation to quit when we're discouraged, coast when we're bored, and rebel when we're angry.

I'm amazed at the story of Joshua, one of the greatest warriors in the Bible. When Moses led the people out of Egypt, he sent twelve spies on recon to look at the Promised Land and bring back a report. Ten of them came back with a dismal analysis that it was impossible for the people who had just been slaves to defeat the giants there (or so they appeared to the doubting ten). But two of them, Joshua and Caleb, believed God and advised Moses to immediately launch the invasion. The ten voted them down, however, and the people spent forty long years camping (and griping) in the desert. Finally, Moses handed the mantle of leadership to Joshua, and he led the Israelites into the land where they defeated their enemies and took residence in the land God had given them. By the end of the account of Joshua's leadership, he was an old man, but he had stayed true to God through thick and thin. At Shechem, God renewed His covenant with His people. Through Joshua, God recounted the story of the conquest and reminded them of His blessings. Then Joshua told them: "Now therefore fear the Lord and serve him in sincerity and in faithfulness. Put away the gods that your fathers served beyond the River and in Egypt, and serve the Lord. And if it is evil in your eyes to serve the Lord, choose this day whom you will serve, whether the gods your fathers served in the region beyond the River, or the gods of the Amorites in whose land you dwell. But as for me and my house, we will serve the Lord" (Joshua 24:14-15). In other words, you can make your own choices. I've made mine. Even if none of you choose to follow God, my family and I will.

There's another hero in this story . . . it's the other spy who believed God so long before: Caleb. In some ways, he's even more remarkable than Joshua because he wasn't chosen as the national leader, and he didn't have the platform given to Joshua, but he didn't pout and slink away. Even as an old man, he wasn't ready to find a comfortable chair, buy a boat, or spend every day on the golf course. He was still in the fight! He claimed his inheritance. He reminded Joshua of God's promise to him: "And Moses swore on that day, saying, 'Surely the land on which your foot has trodden shall be an inheritance for you and your children forever, because you have wholly followed the Lord my God'" (Joshua 14:9). And then Caleb announced:

And now, behold, the Lord has kept me alive, just as he said, these forty-five years since the time that the Lord spoke this word to Moses, while Israel walked in the wilderness. And now, behold, I am this day eighty-five years old. I am still as strong today as I was in the day that Moses sent me; my strength now is as my strength was then, for war and for going and coming. So now give me this hill country of which the Lord spoke on that day, for you heard on that day how the Anakim were there, with great fortified cities. It may be that the Lord will be with me, and I shall drive them out just as the Lord said." (vv. 10-12)

Can't you hear the old guy growl, "Give me that mountain!"? And he took it. Years ago, I heard Pastor Chuck Smith, the founder of the Calvary Chapel movement, say that retirement isn't taught (or even suggested) anywhere in the Scriptures, and God's call to follow wherever He leads doesn't end at a certain age. We may change careers, perhaps to unpaid volunteer service, but we still follow God's voice. Pastor Chuck said that he hoped God would call him home when he was preaching. He thought that would be a glorious way to die . . . even if it would cause more than a little alarm among those in the congregation that day—especially the visitors! Caleb and Pastor Chuck were made from the same mold.

We may change careers, perhaps to unpaid volunteer service, but we still follow God's voice.

As I've thought about Pastor Chuck's hope, it has helped me stay on track with Jesus because I don't want to pass from this life to the next while I'm doing something irrelevant or stupid. I know I can go at any time, and I want to walk into Jesus' arms from a place of joyful obedience, not covered with shame for something I was doing at the time.

God isn't a vendor to give us products or services we want. Our challenge is to align our agendas with His, not expect Him to align with ours. After Stephen was stoned to death not long after Jesus was raised and ascended back to heaven, believers were severely persecuted in Jerusalem and the surrounding area after a pogrom led by the ringleader, Saul of Tarsus, later known as Paul. They ran for their lives, but they didn't wallow in self-pity and blame God for what happened to them. They realized this was exactly what Jesus had predicted on the night before He was arrested: "If the world hates you, know that it has hated me before it hated you. If you were of the world, the world would love you as its own; but because you are not of the world, but I chose you out of the world, therefore the world hates you. Remember the word that I said to you: 'A servant is not greater than his master.' If they persecuted me, they will also persecute you. If they kept my word, they will also keep yours" (John 15:18-20).

The Christian life isn't what a lot of people think it is. Sure, there are "precious and magnificent promises," but these are given in the context of selfless sacrifice and humble obedience. This doesn't mean we never take a break to enjoy life. Jesus often took His disciples on retreats to rest and regroup, but those excursions weren't because they gave up on the mission—they were getting ready for the next phase of the mission. Jesus, the perfect man, lived a full but balanced life, alternating between intense engagement and times of rest. That's a good pattern for all of us. Joshua and Caleb ended well. They endured times of struggle and a long, long season of waiting for God's promises to be fulfilled, but at the end of their lives, they were still trusting, still moving forward, still making a difference. That's the kind of legacy I want to leave behind . . . and if you've read this far in the book, I'm sure that's your vision for your legacy, too.

SPIRITUAL CONDITIONING

Athletes condition their bodies to perform at their very best, and we need to follow their example to condition our souls. The weight training, running mile after mile, swimming laps, healthy food, and sleep prepare the athlete for the competition, the moment when physical and mental conditioning pays off. In the same way, we study the Scriptures, pray, spend time in honest relationships, give, love, and serve because one day—it's inevitable—we'll get the phone call, we'll hear a doctor's diagnosis, a child or grandchild will be in trouble, or some other traumatic event will occur. If we aren't ready, we'll panic, become emotionally paralyzed, or try to run away.

Sung and I married in 2004. We wanted to have children right away, but, as I mentioned earlier, we had trouble getting pregnant. Both of us went through some tests, and the doctors determined that I wasn't producing enough sperm. I had to have surgery—which was unutterably painful—but it didn't work. We were disappointed and frustrated. Later, I had to make a business trip to Belgium, and Sung wanted to go along. When my meetings were over, with nothing more than our backpacks, we took trains to

France and then into Italy. We went to the Italian west coast to a string of five beautiful little towns where the mountains meet the sea, called Cinque Terra. In one of the towns, I asked a lady if she could direct us where we might spend a few nights. She spoke in a combination of Italian and English, but we figured out that she was offering us a room in her home. It was right on the water, very picturesque. She cooked breakfast for us each morning, and we loved staying there.

We returned home, and a couple of weeks later, Sung told me she missed her period. We were guardedly hopeful. She purchased a pregnancy test, and it was positive! It was Mother's Day, 2005. A visit to the doctor confirmed the pregnancy. We were ecstatic! A few weeks later, she went back for an ultrasound. Sung had sensed that God was going to give us a double blessing of twins, and the ultrasound showed two developing babies. We told everybody how God was blessing us. We couldn't wait for the babies to arrive, and we made grand plans for the nursery. We named the two girls Tehya and Angelina.

At the sixth-month checkup, the doctor told us that one of the twins was growing faster than the other, but there was nothing to worry about. A few weeks later, another ultrasound showed the disparity in the twins' growth was even more pronounced. The doctor's concern was becoming palpable, so we were referred to a specialist for another procedure and a second opinion. When the nurse had the ultrasound probe gliding across Sung's belly on a sea of gel, we hoped she was going to say, "Yes, one of the twins is a little bigger than the other, but that's not a problem. Everything looks great!" But she didn't say that. In fact, she didn't say anything. The procedure usually lasted about an hour, but after only ten minutes, the nurse stopped. She tried to avoid looking at me, but I could see the anxiety on her face. I asked, "What's the matter?"

She had obviously been trained to avoid answering questions like this, so she immediately blurted out, "Nothing. Nothing at all." She turned and walked toward the door. "I'll get the doctor, and we'll be right back." She didn't have to say anything. I knew.

A few minutes later, the doctor walked in and put the probe on Sung's stomach. After only a minute or two, he looked at us and said, "I'm sorry, but one of the twins has passed away." I felt like a mule kicked me in the chest.

The doctor wasn't finished with the bad news. He explained that the twins were mono-amniotic, and cells from the dead child would have an inverse impact on the one that was still alive. "Undoubtedly," he said sadly, "a lot of damage has already been done to the living child." He paused for a second and then told us, "Most parents would abort at this point."

We were stunned. Sung and I wanted these children so much. We were confused as well as shocked. She started weeping, and I wept with her. The doctor explained that the living baby may not make it until birth, and if she did, she may die soon after she was born, and if she lived longer than that, she would probably have devastating birth defects.

At the time, I'd only been a Christian for about four years, so this was the first big test of my faith. I told him, "We're not most parents. We're not going to abort our baby."

When we left and drove home, both of us were still crying. At that point in my spiritual journey, I'd relied heavily on our pastor at Cornerstone Church in Howell, New Jersey, for feedback and advice. I tried several times to call Pastor Chris, but there was no answer. I sped to the church where there was usually a lot going on at that time during the week, but there wasn't a single car in the parking lot. I sensed God whisper to me, "Are you going to look for a person to comfort you, or are you going to depend on Me?"

We drove home, and we began to process the terrible news. A few years earlier, Jeremy Camp had released a single called "I Still Believe." He had written it after his wife, Melissa, died from cancer. We put the song on repeat:

> I still believe in Your faithfulness
> I still believe in Your truth
> I still believe in Your holy Word
> even when I don't see, I still believe
>
> Though the questions still fog up my mind
> with promises I still seem to bear
> even when answers slowly unwind
> it's my heart I see You prepare
> but it's now that I feel Your grace fall like rain
> from every fingertip, washing away my pain[32]

Sung and I returned to see the specialist the next day. We asked if there were any options, and he told us he might be able to get Sung into a clinical trial at The Children's Hospital in Philadelphia. That was good news . . . and bad news. It would require a lot of time away from the office. I was a rising sales star. I had a lot of really important things to do, and I couldn't afford to be gone from the office as much as this would require. Thankfully, that selfish thought quickly disintegrated as I thought about what was most important.

For the next several weeks, we commuted once a week from our home in New Jersey about an hour and a half each way to the hospital in Philadelphia. The procedures took much of the day. In the first examination, the pediatric cardiologist told us that Tehya's heart was in a very precarious condition. Her arteries and veins were weak, and her heart could stop at any moment. He said that he didn't expect her to be living when we were scheduled to see him a week later.

The pediatric neurologist came in the room, conducted some tests, and then showed us two brain scans. He compared a normal baby's brain to Tehya's scan, and he pointed to hers. "Do you see the spots on her brain? They are from blood clots entering her brain from the tissue from the other baby. If she lives, she'll be a special needs child."

We had prayed about all eventualities, and we were content that if God gave us a child with special needs, we'd love that child to the utmost. We were committed to trust Him, no matter the outcome.

Those weeks were strangely both painful and peaceful. The reality of the situation wasn't lost on us. We weren't in denial about the huge problems, but we were convinced that God would give us grace and strength to trust Him. Our last appointment in Philadelphia was almost at the end of the nine months. This was going to be the final, complete analysis from all the doctors. We sat in a room with us on one side of the table and the doctors on the other. The pediatric cardiologist went first. He showed us two X-rays, one from a few weeks before and one taken that day. He said, "You can see that her heart today is much healthier than it was before. In fact, it looks perfectly healthy, functioning just as it should."

The pediatric neurologist took his turn. "Mr. and Mrs. Bowen, I don't know how to explain this. It has never happened in my years of practice as a doctor." He pointed to two brain scans and said, "The spots on the scan we took a few weeks ago gave me a lot of concern. I was convinced she would have severe developmental abnormalities, but the spots are gone." He pointed to the scan taken that day and said, "Look at this. Not a single spot. She has a perfectly healthy brain."

I wanted to jump up from my chair, throw my arms up, and yell, "Hallelujah!" but there was one more person on the other side of the table: the case manager. He took a deep breath and told us, "We didn't expect this outcome. I've reviewed all the tests and scans, as well as the history from your previous doctors, and I can tell you that your surviving baby is perfectly healthy. Go home and enjoy the next week or two until your baby is born."

Sung went into labor on Christmas day. I tell people that the Lord didn't want to share His birthday, so Tehya was born the next day. Today, she's one of the most wonderful, smart, eager young women I know. She has a deep heart for God, and He's using her to touch many lives.

Of course, things don't always turn out like this. People aren't always healed of diseases, a job offer doesn't come, a strained relationship doesn't mend, and our hopes are dashed. God will always fulfill His promises, but seldom in the time or the way we expect.

Tests come our way. In fact, I've learned to see every moment of every day as a test. When I encounter heartaches in our family or setbacks in business, God is strengthening my faith to trust Him as I walk through them. When I face prolonged times when prayers aren't answered and life is a strain, God assures me that He's building my faith and endurance. And when I experience the overflow of God's generosity in blessings, He reminds me that all good things come from Him—and thankfulness, not pride in my accomplishments, is the right response.

Tests come our way. In fact, I've learned to see every moment of every day as a test.

The victory is sometimes in magnificent answers to prayer, but far more often, the victory is God giving us courageous faith to trust Him in times of difficulty and doubt. Professor J. I. Packer has, I believe, the perspective that enables us to trust God through anything life throws at us:

> This is what all the work of grace aims at—an ever deeper knowledge of God, and an ever closer fellowship with Him. Grace is God drawing us sinners closer and closer to Himself.
> How does God in grace prosecute this purpose? Not by shielding us from assault by the world, the flesh, and the devil, nor by protecting us from burdensome and frustrating circumstances, nor yet by shielding us from troubles created by our own temperament and psychology; but rather by exposing us to all these things, so as to overwhelm us with a sense of our own inadequacy, and to

drive us to cling to Him more closely. This is the ultimate reason, from our standpoint, why God fills our lives with troubles and perplexities of one sort and another—it is to ensure that we shall learn to hold Him fast.

They say that those who never make mistakes never make anything; certainly, these men made mistakes, but through their mistakes God taught them to know His grace, and to cleave to Him in a way that would never have happened otherwise. Is your trouble a sense of failure? the knowledge of having made some ghastly mistake? Go back to God; His restoring grace waits for you.[33]

Are you "overwhelmed with your own inadequacy"? If you are, you're in the right place—at the bottom so that you can only look up to see God's grace, love, wisdom, and strength . . . and His sometimes inscrutable path for your life.

YOUR OBITUARY

When I think about the impact of my life, I can get lost in the weeds of daily decisions. It helps me to consider the end, to imagine what will be written on my tombstone and in my obituary. When people ask my family about me, what will Sung and the children tell them?

When we lived in Minnesota a few years ago, early one morning I was driving on Pilot Knob Road to a men's Bible study. About a half-mile from River Valley Church, I saw skid marks on the road, and where they hit the curb, there was a memorial with flowers and a candle. We lived in a relatively small community, so I thought surely I would have heard about someone being killed in an accident, but I knew nothing about it. After the study, I went home and Googled the incident. I learned that the night before two young men had veered into the oncoming lane and were hit head-on by a truck. It was the truck's skid marks on the road. Both of the young men died instantly. I looked up their names on social media to see what was important to them right before they died. I saw pictures of parties, cruel memes, and some snarky political posts . . . that was the last impression those two young men left on the world. I felt really sad as I thought about them.

I realized it could have been me. If I'd died the night before or that morning on the way to the church, what would have been my last impressions on people? If I'm going to be reckless, I want to live in reckless love and obedience to God. All day every day.

God hasn't called me to be the apostle Paul or Dietrich Bonhoeffer or Billy Graham or Martin Luther or any other giant in the faith, but He's called me to be faithful to Him and make a difference every day in the lives of the people around me. My minutes, hours, days, weeks, and years are the equity God has put in my hands, and it's up to me to invest them wisely for the greatest return—not for my brokerage account or my prestige, but for Christ's fame and glory. As a good investor, I need to do my research, consider the returns I'm getting, and make adjustments along the way to have the greatest impact.

How are you investing your life?

THINK ABOUT IT:

1. Which of the two faithful spies inspires you more, Joshua or Caleb? Explain your answer.

2. How would you define and describe "the victorious Christian life"?

3. Do you agree or disagree that God may call us to change careers, but retirement isn't a biblical concept? How has your perspective changed, if it has at all?

4. What are some circumstances that have caused people you know to be so discouraged that they want to quit on their walk of faith? To be so bored that they only coast through life? Or to be so angry they rebel against God? Which of these is a temptation for you?

5. Look at the lyrics for "I Still Believe" and consider they were written when Jeremy Camp's wife died. What would you have to believe in the core of your soul to believe like that?

6. Take a few minutes to consider what you'd want your epitaph to be, and write it down.

7. What's the next step in your walk with Jesus? When, where, how, and with whom will you take it?

Endnotes

1. Jim Collins, "Level 5 Leadership: The Triumph of Humility and Fierce Resolve," *Harvard Business Review*, January 2001, https://hbr.org/2001/01/level-5-leadership-the-triumph-of-humility-and-fierce-resolve-2

2. These traits are adapted from "The Signs of an Emotionally Emasculated Man," Joseph Mattera, April 25, 2016, https://josephmattera.org/the-signs-of-an-emotionally-emasculated-man/

3. Jocko Willink and Leif Babin, *Extreme Ownership* (New York: McMillan, 2015), pp. 14, 26.

4. Augustine, *Sermons* 191.1

5. *Making Disciples*, "Part 1 Equipping Series," Larry DiSiome," pp. 84-85. Available at www.canyoncalvary.com.

6. John White, *The Fight* (Downers Grove, IL: InterVarsity Press, 1976), pp. 87-88.

7. Cited in "Navy SEAL Adam Brown Battled Taliban to the Death" by Scott S. Smith, *Investor's Business Daily*, May 23, 2014 and "How an Addict Became a Navy SEAL and a Nightmare for the Taliban" by Blake Stilwell, *The Mighty*, April 29, 2020, https://www.wearethemighty.com/mighty-trending/navy-seal-adam-brown-fearless/

8. Henri Nouwen, *Bread for the Journey* (New York: HarperCollins, 1997), p. 212.

9. *Braveheart*, scene posted on YouTube, https://www.youtube.com/watch?v=h2vW-rr9ibE

10. *The Finest Hour* opening scene clip: https://www.youtube.com/watch?v=-mYfi50ZDUYhe

11. Ken Dilanian and Mike Hixenbaugh, "Heartbroken Dad Demands Change in SEAL Training after Son's Death," NBC News, June 10, 2016, https://www.nbcnews.com/news/us-news/heartbroken-dad-demands-change-navy-seal-training-after-son-s-n589101

12. Kyle Idleman, *Gods at War* (Grand Rapids: Zondervan, 2018), p. 27.

13. David Foster Wallace, "This Is Water," Kenyon College, 2005, https://fs.blog/2012/04/david-foster-wallace-this-is-water/

14. Tim Keller, *Counterfeit Gods* (New York: Penguin, 2010), p. xxvi.

15. J. I. Packer, *Knowing God* (Downers Grove, IL: InterVarsity Press, 1973), pp. 187-188.

16. Morgan DeBusk-Lane, "Social Identity in the Military," Penn State Applied Psychology, February 27, 2015, https://sites.psu.edu/aspsy/2015/02/27/social-identity-in-the-military/

17. C. S. Lewis, "The Weight of Glory," a message given at the Church of St. Mary the Virgin, Oxford, England, June 8, 1942, https://www.wheelersburg.net/Downloads/Lewis%20Glory.pdf

18. N. T. Wright, *For All God's Worth: True Worship and the Calling of the Church* (Grand Rapids: Eerdmans, 1997), p. 1.

19. Peter Wehner, "The Deepening Crisis in Evangelical Christianity," *The Atlantic*, July 5, 2019, https://www.theatlantic.com/ideas/archive/2019/07/evangelical-christians-face-deepening-crisis/593353/

20. For instance, see FiveThirtyEight: https://fivethirtyeight.com/features/more-and-more-americans-arent-religious-why-are-dem-ocrats-ignoring-these-voters/ and Pew Research: https://www.pewresearch.org/fact-tank/2017/05/04/though-still-conserva-tive-young-evangelicals-are-more-liberal-than-their-elders-on-some-issues/

21. Timothy Keller, "A Better Resurrection," March 27, 2005, https://gospelinlife.com/downloads/a-better-resurrection-easter-5408/

22. "First Navy SEAL Killed in Iraq," https://americasmightywar-riors.org/about-marc/

23. 7 Startling Facts: An Up Close Look at Church Attendance in America, *Outreach*, April 10, 2018, https://churchleaders.com/ pastors/pastor-articles/139575-7-startling-facts-an-up-close-look-at-church-attendance-in-america.html

24. Rodney Stark, *The Triumph of Christianity: How the Jesus Movement Became the World's Largest Religion* (New York: HarperOne, 2011), 114-119.

25. Eusebius, *Eccl. Hist.* 7.22.7–10.

26. Glen Scrivener, "Responding to Pandemics: 4 Lessons from Church History," Gospel Coalition, March 16, 2020, https:// www.thegospelcoalition.org/article/4-lessons-church-history/

27. Rodney Stark, *The Rise of Christianity,* https://www.human-science.org/docs/Stark%20(1996)%20Rise%20of%20 Christianity%201-2.pdf

28. John Ortberg, *The Life You've Always Wanted* (Grand Rapids: Zondervan, 2002), p. 89.

29. Robert O'Neill, *The Operator* (New York: Simon & Schuster, 2017), p. 95.

30. Alan Redpath, *The Making of a Man of God* (Grand Rapids: Fleming H. Revell, 1962), p. 44.

31. Alan Redpath, *Victorious Christian Living* (Grand Rapids: Fleming H. Revel, 2013), p. 18.

32. Jeremy Camp, "I Still Believe," *Stay*, 2002, BEC Recordings, 2002.

33. J. I. Packer, *Knowing God* (Downers Grove, IL: InterVarsity Press, 1973), pp. 226-228.

Acknowledgments

This book would not have been possible without the love and grace of Christ, my rock.

I'm so grateful for . . .

My wife Sung, who has loved me when I didn't deserve it and modeled for me what it means to be committed.

My children and grandchildren, for their love and patience as God continues to mold and shape me into His image.

Mr. Dave Dudley, who has loved me and continues to love me as his own son.

Everyone at our companies. Thank you for being patient with me over the years and letting me serve you, for being a part of our amazing companies, and for showing up every day and being in the business of serving and loving people well.

Pat Springle and his amazing team, who helped make this book a reality.

The members of our armed services, who have sacrificed and continue to sacrifice each day to protect the freedoms we enjoy.

All those who are mentioned in this book for being a part of a beautiful story of love and redemption.

And finally, to those reading this book, my prayer is that God speaks to you personally and that you will embrace the fact that you are a work in progress. Keep your eyes on Him, and keep pushing forward.

Using *The Brave* in Groups and Classes

The Brave is designed for individual study, small groups, and classes. The best way to absorb and apply these principles is for each person to individually study and answer the questions at the end of each chapter, and then discuss them in a group environment.

Order enough copies of the book for each person to have a copy. A recommended schedule for a small group or class might be:

WEEK 1

Introduce the material. As a group leader, tell your story of learning to trust God, share your hopes for the group, and provide books for each person. Encourage people to read the assigned chapter each week and answer the questions.

WEEKS 2–11

Each week, introduce the topic for the week and share a story of how God has used the principles in your life. Lead people through a discussion of the questions at the end of the chapter.

PERSONALIZE EACH LESSON

Don't feel pressured to cover every question in your group discussions. You may have time for all of them, but if not, pick out three or four that had the biggest impact on you, and focus on those, or ask people in the group to share their responses to the questions that meant the most to them that week.

Make sure you personalize the principles and applications. At least once in each group meeting, add your own story to illustrate a particular point.

Make the Scriptures come alive. Far too often, we read the Bible like it's a phone book, with little or no emotion. Paint a vivid picture for people. Provide insights about the risk and the power of authentic relationships, and help those in your group sense the emotions of specific people in each scene.

FOCUS ON APPLICATION

The questions at the end of each chapter and your encouragement to group members to be authentic will help your group take big steps to apply the principles they're learning. Share how you are applying the principles in particular chapters each week, and encourage them to take steps of growth, too.

THREE TYPES OF QUESTIONS

If you've led groups for a few years, you already understand the importance of using open questions to stimulate discussion. Three types of questions are *limiting, leading,* and *open.* Many of the questions at the end of each lesson are open questions.

- *Limiting questions* focus on an obvious answer, such as, "What does Jesus call himself in John 10:11?" They don't stimulate reflection or discussion. If you want to use questions like these, follow them with thought-provoking, open questions.

- *Leading questions* require the listener to guess what the leader has in mind, such as, "Why did Jesus use the metaphor of a shepherd in John 10?" (He was probably alluding to a passage in Ezekiel, but many people don't know that.) The teacher who asks a leading question has a definite answer in mind. Instead of asking this kind of question, you should just teach the point and perhaps ask an open question about the point you have made.

■ *Open questions* usually don't have right or wrong answers. They stimulate thinking, and they are far less threatening because the person answering doesn't risk ridicule for being wrong. These questions often begin with "Why do you think . . .?" or "What are some reasons that . . .?" or "How would you have felt in that situation?"

PREPARATION

As you prepare to teach this material in a group, consider these steps:

1. Carefully and thoughtfully read the book. Make notes, highlight key sections, quotes, or stories, and complete the reflection section at the end of each chapter. This will familiarize you with the entire scope of the content.

2. As you prepare for each week's group, read the corresponding chapter again and make additional notes.

3. Tailor the amount of content to the time allotted. You may not have time to cover all the questions, so pick the ones that are most pertinent.

4. Add your own stories to personalize the message and add impact.

5. Before and during your preparation, ask God to give you wisdom, clarity, and power. Trust Him to use your group to change people's lives.

6. Most people will get far more out of the group if they read the chapter and complete the reflection each week. Order books before the group or class begins or after the first week.

About the Author

Michael Bowen is the founder and president of BOM JITSU, a martial arts academy in Castle Rock, Colorado. He has been actively involved in various aspects of martial arts since he was thirteen years old. As a teenager, he practiced Kuk Sool Won, a Korean martial art, and was drawn to the physical and mental aspect of the sport.

In 2015, Michael began his Jiu Jitsu journey under Larry Glines (a Black Belt under Robert Drysdale) at the Fountain of Youth Jiu Jitsu Academy. As an active surfer, adventure racer, and martial arts practitioner, Michael was seeking something more challenging that he could use to train with his children. Larry helped shape Michael's fundamental principles and love for Jiu Jitsu. After moving to Lakeville, Minnesota, in 2018, Michael started training at Rio Jitsu (GFTeam) and had several outstanding coaches, including João Tavares Marinho, Jose Luis Varella, and Hiago Adao, who continued sharpening his fundamentals and helped him define the skills for competing. He also completed Jiu Jitsu mentorship with Gutemberg Pereira.

Michael has competed in multiple national competitions. He moved back to Castle Rock, Colorado, to open BOM JITSU Academy with Black Belt Coach Guilherme Cordiviola. Their love for the sport is infectious, and they are dedicated to shape the lives of students through a world-class integrative Jiu Jitsu program. He explains his approach, "Whether participants are just beginning or they've been train-

ing for years, our hope is that those involved will grow spiritually, physically, mentally, and emotionally with our family of athletes." Michael and his wife Sung are creating a program designed to reach at-risk youth worldwide through mentorship utilizing Jiu Jitsu and faith.

Michael and Sung have five children—Arthur, Bradley, Tehya, Caleb, and Micalah—and three grandchildren—Benjamin, Jack, and Adelaide.

Resources

To order more copies of this book, go to **uncommondisciple.com** or **amazon.com**

UNCOMMON DISCIPLE

Uncommon Disciple helps everyday men build an eternal legacy. We believe God created men to be leaders of honor, integrity, strength, and grace. The problem is that while many men desire to become all God has called them to be,

they burn out or become distracted along the way. Fathers desire to be godly examples to their children, but they often carry the guilt and shame of their failures. Young singles may be full of vision, but they usually lack the wisdom and endurance to stay on course to fulfillment. These all-too-common stories are the reason we believe God is calling us to build uncommon disciples.

Much more than resources, conferences, and community groups, Uncommon Disciple is a movement of men seeking sustainable life-change.

For more information about joining this movement, go to: **uncommondisciple.com**

BOM JITSU

Bom Jitsu is a Brazilian Jiu Jitsu and fitness center located in the Denver metro area. As a Grappling Fight Team affiliate, Bom Jitsu

gives everyone from kids and beginners to world class fighters a place to develop physical, mental, emotional, and spiritual growth. The training mat is where many life lessons are learned and self-discovery often begins. Bom athletes don't settle for average; they operate under the philosophy that all people, from at-risk youth to successful entrepreneurs, can have the opportunity to live fearlessly wherever life takes them.

For more information, go to: **bomjitsu.com**